Understanding Evil

Understanding

evil

Alan Ames

The decree of the *Congregation of the Propagation of the Faith*, A.A.S 58, 1186 (approved by Pope Paul VI on October 14, 1966) states that the Nihil Obstat and Imprimatur are no longer required on publications that deal with private revelations, provided that they contain nothing contrary to faith and morals.

The publisher recognizes and accepts that the final authority regarding the events described in this book rests with the Holy See of Rome, to whose judgement we willingly submit.

Sections of this book may not be copied without permission of the author.

© 2013 Carver Alan Ames

Layout and design: Andreas Zureich, Germany.
Cover photo: © Rudolf Baier, Germany.

ISBN 978-0-9820329-7-8

DEDICATION *This book is dedicated to my dear friend Sr. Claude McNamara RSM, Perth, West Australia and to Moritz Schneider, Bavaria, Germany...who has shown me the true face of Christ in his suffering.*

CONTENTS

Introduction	13	**Compromising**	27
		Jesus	27
Foreword	15	Mother Mary	27
		Confused	27
Understanding Evil	21	Jesus	27
		St. Michael the Archangel	28
Actions	21	**Corruption**	29
God the Father	21	Jesus	29
Angels	21	Mother Mary	29
God the Father	21	**Deceptions**	29
Jesus	22	Jesus	29
St. Raphael Archangel	22	God the Father	30
St. Michael the Archangel	22	Mother Mary	30
Attacks of Evil	23	**Defeated**	31
God the Father	23	Jesus	31
Jesus	23	Mother Mary	31
St. Paul	24	**Denial of God**	32
Bitter Fruit	24	St. James the Lesser	32
Jesus	24	**Denying Good**	32
Blinded by Evil	24	Jesus	32
God the Father	24	**Destruction**	32
Jesus	25	God the Father	32
St. Clare	26	Jesus	33
Christmas	26	Mother Mary	33
Jesus	26	**Distractions**	33
St. Gabriel the Archangel	26	St. Teresa of Avila	33
		Drugs	35
		God the Father	35

Easter	35	**Force**	45
Jesus	35	*Jesus*	45
Mother Mary	36	*Mother Mary*	45
St. Peter the Apostle	36	**Freedom**	46
Empires	36	*Jesus*	46
Jesus	36	*God the Father*	48
Eternity	37	**Gentleness**	48
God the Father	37	*Jesus*	48
Jesus	37	**Goodness**	49
Equality	37	*God the Father*	49
God the Father	37	*Jesus*	49
Families	38	*Mother Mary*	50
Mother Mary	38	**Hatred**	50
False Humour	38	*God the Father*	50
Jesus	38	*Jesus*	50
Fear	38	**Hell**	51
God the Father	38	*God the Father*	51
Jesus	39	**Justifying Evil**	51
Holy Spirit	39	*God the Father*	51
Mother Mary	40	*Jesus*	51
St. Benedict	40	**Keeping Evil at Bay**	52
St. Aloyisius	41	*God the Father*	52
St. Blaise	41	*Mother Mary*	52
St. Andrew	41	*Jesus*	52
Fighting Evil	41	**Led by Evil**	53
God the Father	41	*God the Father*	53
Mother Mary	42	*Jesus*	53
St. Michael Archangel	42	*Mother Mary*	53
Foolish	43	**Life**	54
Jesus	43	*God the Father*	54
Holy Spirit	44	*Jesus*	54
Mother Mary	45	**Living in God**	55
		God the Father	55
		Jesus	55

Loving Hearts..................	56
God the Father	56
St. Michael the Archangel	56
Marriage.....................	57
Jesus	57
Mother Mary	57
Negotiating with Evil.........	58
Jesus	58
New Age.....................	58
Jesus	58
Offending God...............	58
Jesus	58
Open to Evil..................	60
God the Father	60
Jesus	60
Mother Mary	61
St. John the Baptist	61
Peace.......................	62
God the Father	62
Jesus	62
Pleasure.....................	62
Jesus	62
Politics......................	63
God the Father	63
Jesus	63
St. John the Baptist	63
Prayer......................	64
God the Father	64
Mother Mary	64
Pride.......................	64
Jesus	64
Priesthood...................	65
God the Father	65
Jesus	65
Mother Mary	66
Recognizing Evil.............	66
God the Father	66
Selfishness...................	66
Jesus	66
Sexual Relationships..........	67
Jesus	67
Mother Mary	68
St. Columban	68
Suffering	69
God the Father	69
Jesus	69
St. Cornelius	70
Superstitions	70
Jesus	70
The taking of Life.............	71
God the Father	71
Jesus	71
Temptations.................	71
God the Father	71
Jesus	71
Terrorism	72
God the Father	72
Jesus	72
St. Teresa of Avila	72
The Church	73
Jesus	73
Mother Mary	73
St. Agnes	73
St. Edmund	74

The Face of Evil	74	Delivered by the Cross	85
Jesus	74		
Holy Spirit	74	**Accepting Crosses**	86
Mother Mary	74	*God the Father*	86
The Grasp of Evil	75	*Jesus*	86
Jesus	75	*Holy Spirit*	86
Holy Spirit	75	**Barriers**	87
Mother Mary	75	*St. Benedict*	87
The Reign of Evil	76	**Blessing**	87
God the Father	76	*God the Father*	87
Jesus	76	*Jesus*	87
Mother Mary	76	*Mother Mary*	88
The Word of God	77	*St. John of the Cross*	88
God the Father	77	**Blindness**	88
Tool of Evil	78	*Jesus*	88
Jesus	78	**Carrying the Cross**	89
True Power	78	*God the Father*	89
God the Father	78	*Jesus*	89
Jesus	79	*Mother Mary*	91
St. Michael Archangel	79	*St. Paul*	91
St. Thomas the Apostle	79	*St. Teresa of Avila*	91
St. Louis	80	*St. John of the Cross*	92
Union	80	*St. Stephen*	92
Jesus	80	**Comfort**	93
War	80	*Jesus*	93
God the Father	80	**Courage**	93
Jesus	81	*God the Father*	93
Holy Spirit	82	**Difficulties**	93
Weakness	82	*Jesus*	93
God the Father	82	*St. Theresa of Avila*	94
Jesus	82	**Darkness**	95
Mother Mary	82	*Jesus*	95
St. Teresa of Avila	83		
Wronged	83		
God the Father	83		

Embrace the Cross	95	**In the Garden**	106
God the Father	95	Jesus	106
Jesus	96	St. Peter Apostle	107
Mother Mary	97	St. Theresa (The little Flower)	107
St. John of the Cross	97	**Looking at the Cross**	108
Forgiveness	97	Jesus	108
Jesus	97	St. John Apostle	109
Mother Mary	98	St. Mary Magdala	109
St. Helena	98	St. John of the Cross	109
From the Cross	98	**Love of the Cross**	109
Jesus	98	Jesus	109
Faith	99	St. John the Apostle	110
Jesus	99	St. John of the Cross	110
Giving	99	**Mercy**	110
Jesus	99	Jesus	110
Guilt	100	Holy Spirit	111
God the Father	100	Mother Mary	111
Heart of the Cross	100	St. Benedict	111
Jesus	100	**More Crosses**	111
St. Paul	101	Jesus	111
St. Margaret Mary	101	**Offering**	111
Heavy Crosses	102	Jesus	111
God the Father	102	St. Mary Magdela	112
Jesus	102	**Proclaim**	112
Mother Mary	103	St. John the Baptist	112
St. John of the Cross	104	**Rewarded**	112
St. Andrew	104	Jesus	112
St. Francis Xavier	104	Mother Mary	113
Holy Week/Good Friday	105	**Salvation**	113
Jesus	105	God the Father	113
Mother Mary	105	Jesus	113
Humility	106		
Jesus	106		
Mother Mary	106		

Shadow of the Cross	**114**
God the Father	114
Jesus	114
St. Andrew	114
Suffering of and with The Lord	**115**
God the Father	115
Jesus	115
Mother Mary	117
St. John of the Cross	117
St. Lucy	118
The Eucharist	**118**
God the Father	118
Jesus	118
The Sign	**119**
Jesus	119
Mother Mary	119
St. John of the Cross	119
Touched	**119**
St. Helena	119
Victory	**120**
God the Father	120
Jesus	120
St. John of the Cross	121
St. Michael the Archangel	121
Wounded for Love	**121**
Jesus	121

Letters	**123**
Let Your Faith Define You	123
Appropriateness of receiving the Eucharist by Catholics who support abortion	124
Christmas Message	128
Do Not Fear Persecution	129
In Love	132
Yes, that is very Christian	133
Catholicism under attack	138
Defending the Church	140
Called to Forgive	143
Atheism	145
The Other Side of the Coin	149
On Prayer	151
The Acceptance of Sin	152
Christmas Message	155
Protestant Discussions	157
No More Than Our Duty	163
The Standard of Christ	164
The Seal That Cannot Be Broken	166
A Warning	168
The Christmas Gift	170
The Year Ahead	172
Conscience and Faith	172
United	174
The Holy Time of Easter	176
Christmas Message	177
Whenever God Touches a Life	177
I Am Love	179
He is with us	180

INTRODUCTION

WE ALL know that life has its ups and downs, its good days and bad days, its light and its dark. That is life, and we learn from how we respond to what comes our way. That's what life is all about, that's why we're here AND that is why the Father sent us His Son, Jesus. He came to help us learn how to live a fully human life; He came to show us what it is to be fully human and how to live in His love with each other, as we prepare for life eternal.

We no longer see God as being on high, doling out his good things to his lowly creatures down below on earth: that's the Old Testament view of God. Jesus has come as God among us, Emmanuel. We can now rely on God's loving presence all around us, enveloping us.

When humanity surveys the world the first thing we see is all of its flaws. If we were to look at it as if it were a garden, we will see the weeds, the common old daisies and a few beautiful rose bushes scattered, here and there. When God surveys the garden of humanity he sees only beautiful rose bushes, despite all of our shortcomings. God only sees what we can become; God sees our potential. He wants to love that potential into existence; it requires an open heart.

That's where the problem often lies: we close our hearts to the divine life that is already within us. Life is played out on the biggest stage of all – the world, but God doesn't sit back like some disinterested spectator or even as some divine puppeteer effecting good and bad on us. God so longs to be a part of our lives – the good and the bad parts, with His strengthening, healing and forgiving power. He is not far away; He is the Holy Spirit that blows where it wills. We have to open the window and let the Spirit in.

Think of how merciful, loving, forgiving and generous you could ever be and know that God is infinitely more so. To say "God loves me" is obsolete. It's the same as saying "the sun is bright and warm" or "the water is wet". It is what it is; it cannot be anything else. God cannot do anything except love; to BE LOVE, eternally. He invites us to come into that love, let us accept that wonderful invitation.

In this book heaven explains how in God's love mankind can overcome the evil that permeates the world and our lives, the evil that works constantly to stop mankind reaching it's full potential in God. Heaven guides people on how to open their hearts so that people can truly accept God's invitation and be the rose bushes of God's love and the world can be the garden of grace it was created to be.

Fr. Richard Rutkauskas,
Perth, Western Australia, August 2013

FOREWORD

IN THIS book Heaven reveals to mankind where mankind is going wrong and how, through the Cross of Christ, mankind can overcome all evil and be victorious in God's love.

Throughout mankind's existence there has been the evil one and his minions trying to draw mankind away from God. Evil succeeded with Adam and Eve and has had continued success with people because of the same weakness of pride. Since evil seduced Adam and Eve, evil has seduced mankind. Since Cain killed Abel in jealousy people kill one another and are jealous of one another.

From the beginning God has been saying to mankind, if you live to My way you will be happy and at peace. Unfortunately, the response of mankind in general has been to ignore God and to live the worldly way which is filled with the deceptions and snares of evil. Mankind does not seem to learn from its history of suffering and pain and repeats the same mistake over and over of preferring the worldly life to the heavenly life we are called to live; because of this mankind continues to suffer.

It seems very foolish to reject what is good for mankind and embrace what is bad for mankind but in general this is what mankind does. Of course there are many who do try to live the way God asks but so many let the worldly ways infiltrate their lives and so live a weakened or watered down version of the life God calls man to. It is at times, for some, much easier to accept what the world says than to stand against it and when so many live with evil ways in their lives they often become the norm that even some of the faithful accept into life. So evil now becomes part of life.

People frequently comment that they wonder why God lets all the suffering in the world continue, blind to the fact that it is mankind that causes the suffering, not God. People do not see that if we want the suffering to end we have to change and live as God asks us to; live caring and sharing for and with each other. When the world rejects evil the suffering will end as God's heavenly kingdom will reign on earth and in His kingdom there is no pain, no hurt, no suffering. God has explained from the beginning how to live happily, whole and healthy but mankind does not want to hear what He says and so we suffer.

Over and over mankind repeats its denial of God and acceptance of evil. If mankind does the same things over and over expecting a different result then truly mankind is foolish. The only way to have a different result is to live differently – to live to the way of God.

To continue along the path that has been littered with wars, famines, pestilence and disasters seems to be what mankind wants to do, not seeing that path only leads to more of the same. Mankind walks the path of self-destruction and is quick to make excuses for doing so and quick to blame God when things go wrong.

Science and reason are at times distorted to make what is obviously untrue seem to be true. Doing this prevents science and reason reaching their full potential as at times they are nothing more than weapons evil uses to hurt and confuse mankind. The altering of, and interfering with, conception, the manipulating of life, the use of aborted babies in experiments and in treatments, the development of weapons used to kill, the destruction of the environment, the abuse of animals, the development of entertaining technology full of violence and immorality and many, many more ways. Until science accepts the existence of God and embraces His moral truth into science then it is impossible for science to bring to mankind its full benefit for science can never achieve fullness.

This confused and foolish world we live in have many who believe unless they can explain something or prove something it is not to be believed in. Many scientists seem to think that unless something fits in with their understanding, theories or expectations then it cannot be true. What pride this is. Pride that the evil one manipulates so well so as to increase the disbelief in God. Atheism becomes the way of some scientists who then through false arguments try to lead many into their disbelief in God. How the evil one laughs.

Because someone has a title before their name or letters after it, or has achieved a high standard of learning does not mean a person is wise. Truly some of the most intelligent people are the most unwise of people in the world. I listened to a prominent scientist and atheist on a television debate who boldly declared that nothing was really something. Surely that is foolish.

However, because of their standing, the fine words they use, the seemingly plausible arguments, these people are often listened to and followed.

The media gives some sort of credence to them by often quoting their words as fact.

A fine example is 'Darwin's Theory of Evolution'. Its title states it is a theory yet people use it as fact. TV programs are made based on it. If it is fact should it not be called 'Darwin's Proven Facts of Evolution'? However, it is not proven so it cannot be. Yet, it is declared by many to be proven and true with even educational systems promoting it as fact, not theory.

Evil uses every means possible to draw mankind away from God and into the darkness. The evil one desires to hurt mankind as much as possible and one of the ways he uses is to destroy families. With the break up of families society is weakened and broken and hatred grows amongst people. With no stable society confusion begins to reign in lives and society becomes open to that which is obviously wrong and sinful. Society even promotes and at times enforces into law what is wrong as being the rights of people when in fact they are the wrongs of people. Immorality abounds, greed and selfishness are often encouraged, life is devalued and destroyed at a whim, innocent babies killed because it is the so-called right of the mother to destroy a child if she does not want it. Many promote illegal drugs of addiction as a fun thing to do, as a pleasure all should be able to have, never mind the suffering drugs bring into so many lives other than those who use them.

Families are supposed to be the building stones of society but if those stones are broken or removed society falls apart. That is what is happening today and that is why the world sinks deeper and deeper into the confusion and uncertainty of darkness. Governments often seem to be willing servants of evil in this march to the destruction of morals and true values. Governments and their legal systems listen more to minority groups promoting evil than the majority who at times oppose it. An example is California where the majority opposed so-called 'gay marriage', but their will was ignored by the legal system. So much for democracy!

As a person looks at the world and the evil that abounds it would be easy to despair but people should remember mankind has been delivered from evil by Our Lord, Jesus Christ. The Saviour of mankind has defeated evil. All mankind needs to do is to embrace and accept Our Lord's victory. All mankind needs to do is to live as best it can to the Saviour's way. All mankind needs to do is to hold onto the cross of The Lord, and be secure in His divine victory. It is in doing this each person by God's grace can overcome and defeat evil in their life. The Lord, Jesus, reaches out in love showing mankind that in His pierced heart of love is all the strength, power and grace needed to be part of His divine victory. Mankind, if it chooses wisely and welcomes the victorious king, Jesus Christ, as Lord and Master, will find the world will become the paradise it was created to be once more. The paradise of God's love where love, peace and joy reign supreme.

Now is the time for mankind to walk the right path and no longer walk the path of its history of suffering and pain. Now is the time for mankind to create a new history of true happiness in Our Lord, Jesus. It is possible. It is there for mankind. The victory is mankind's if it chooses to be part of the victory over evil instead of chooses to be the defeated victims of evil. The offer from God is there, it always has been. The offer from God is eternal and glorious. The offer from God surely can only be refused by the foolish who desire to keep suffering. The world and the people on it are called to glory, it is about time we truly answered that call in and through Jesus Christ, Our Lord, and loving Master who loves all and wants all to live in His divine love forever.

God bless,
Alan Ames

UNDERSTANDING EVIL

Actions

God the Father

ALL ACTIONS of love have their rewards just as all actions of evil demand their payment.

THERE IS much to do for God and many are called to do it. There is much to do for God but only a few are prepared to truly accept His call. There is much to do for God and those who do it must join together to help and support each other in a battle of love against evil.

James 4:11 — Do not speak evil of one another.

Angels

God the Father

THE ARCHANGELS are filled with My power to stand against evil and filled with My love to stand against hate. The Archangels, signs of My powerful love.

Psalm 103:20 — Angels mighty in strength and attentive, obedient to every command.

Jesus

Remember there are more good angels and good souls than evil ones.

St. Raphael Archangel

There is an angel of God travelling the road of life with each person, trying to guide and protect that person on their journey.

There is an angel of God travelling the road of life with each person, facing the evil that attacks at every opportunity.

There is an angel of God travelling the road of life with each person, waiting for the person to unite with them in God's love, so that together they can walk in the joy-filled peace of God, fearing no evil and offering all those they meet a guiding hand when needed.

Judges 2:4 — The angel of the lord.

St. Michael the Archangel

Angels of God wait patiently for those on earth to ask for their help in the fight against evil. Every good angel longs to serve God and to serve man in the battle for souls knowing that by God's grace victory is assured.

God's angels watch over each person keeping evil at bay. Sadly, many people let evil in by sinning and pushing their angels away.

God's will is that all mankind be given the opportunity to be saved from evil. When mankind accepts this truth and embrace this opportunity is when mankind will avoid falling into the hands of evil and will avoid being as foolish as some of the angels were.

Attacks of Evil

God the Father

IT IS in the sacraments you will find the grace needed to overcome the attacks of evil.

Jesus

ALL WHO love and serve Me will face fierce opposition; it is to be expected. So do not be surprised when evil attacks.

IN A truly holy life all the attacks of evil lead the person closer to Me not away from Me.

THERE IS a constant battle for souls between good and evil. It is a battle only possible for evil to win if a person accepts evil over good in their life on earth.

EVEN THOUGH evil may destroy the body of those who love Me, it cannot destroy the soul of those who hold onto My love.

EVEN WHEN you are in My presence do not expect evil to leave you in peace. It is in these moments evil makes a special effort to distract you.

NOTHING EVIL can do can stop one who truly loves Me and is truly committed to doing My will.

St. Paul

> As I travelled the world to make the love of Jesus, The Lord, known, I faced many trials and tribulations but each one was overcome by the grace of God. So it will be for all those who endeavour to spread the love of God as evil will do its best to stop them. However, if they trust in God He will give them the grace these people need, just as He gave it to me.
>
> EVIL USES threats, violence, ridicule and abuse to stop those who oppose it so do not be surprised when it happens to you.

Bitter Fruit

Jesus

> THE WORLD will take all it can from people and give them little of true value in return because evil has a grip on the world and this is a bitter fruit of evil.

Blinded by Evil

God the Father

> EVIL BLINDS people by working on their pride and weaknesses so that even the most serious wrong can be accepted as right.
>
> TO SEEK eternal life in heaven should be the desire of all people but because so many have been blinded by evil they only seek to have everything in life on earth.

Jesus

EVIL CORRUPTS the world and in the blindness of pride and self many do not see this.

WHERE THERE is greed there is evil.

WHEN EVIL enters a life often it blinds people to the truth and brings them to see no wrong in their sins. However, on judgement day the wrongs will be clearly seen and regretted but for some the sorrow for sinning will come too late. That is why it is important My followers avoid sin and help others to do the same so the sorrow and repentance comes in this life on earth and the sins do not bring eternal suffering in the next.

THERE ARE many ways evil tries to seduce people into its web of sin but all its ways have one thing in common, they all lead to the same end; eternal suffering in hell. This is true even for the ways which seem to involve little that are wrong or sinful. Because these ways are designed to lead the foolish into bigger and bigger wrongs or to accept more and more sin. Until one day people are blinded to what is wrong and to what is evil and so that they can no longer discern what is right. In this blindness it is then easier for them to be pushed into the chasm of darkness where they stumble and fall into the pit of hell where eternal suffering awaits them.

MANKIND HAS been blinded by evil throughout its history and today it is the same. This blindness has caused great suffering and will continue to do so until mankind sees in Me the way to live and lives to My way.

EVIL TAKES away the consciences of so many so that no longer do they see wrong as wrong.

EVIL LEADS people to do foolish things blinding them so they do not see the idiocy they embrace. All the while evil laughs at the ease at which it can manipulate mankind and lead it into the dark where evil brings suffering to souls.

St. Clare

HOW CAN the wealthy look at the poor and ignore their plight, doing little to help? They can do it because evil has drawn many of the wealthy into self and blinded many of the wealthy with pride.

Christmas

Jesus

HEAVEN AND earth united in Me, God and man in My divinity. Evil defeated forevermore as to mankind I opened heaven's door. All mankind needs to do now is come to Me in a humble bow. Then they will be welcomed inside where I eternally reside. To enjoy in heaven above the glory of My eternal love.

St. Gabriel the Archangel   Christmas Day

PROCLAIM TO the world the Saviour has come and that He will deny none. Proclaim to the world heaven can be theirs if they reject evil and accept, because of Jesus, they are God's heirs. Proclaim to the world The Lord of Love has come to the world from above. Proclaiming to the world this good news know that sanctity will be yours.

Compromising

Jesus

IT IS good to be able to compromise to achieve what is right but a person must never compromise with evil or sin.

UNDER NO circumstances agree with sin because if you do you invite the evil one into your life.

A WISE person is one who denies evil at all times.

Mother Mary

IT IS impossible to reason with evil as evil has nothing in its heart except deceit, hatred and sin.

Confused

Jesus

THE WORLD is a confused place because so many embrace the ways of evil instead of embracing My way of love.

THERE ARE many confused people in the grasp of evil and unless those who love Me take My healing love to these people, many will stay confused.

Hosea 7:3 — in their wickedness.

EVIL TWISTS the minds of many so that what is obviously wrong no longer seems so.

EVIL INFECTS the world and through that infection confuses and blinds people to the truth so that often wrong seems right and right seems wrong.

EVIL HAS no clarity so do not be surprised if those who embrace evil or are used by evil are confused.

THROUGH THE confusion evil brings into life My truth remains unmoved. It is there waiting for all so as to bring the clarity of My love into all lives. All that is needed for this to happen is for Me to receive a true invitation from people and in true love I will respond.

IF CONFUSION reigns then evil is near. If uncertainty abounds then evil is working. If doubt lives then evil is succeeding in confusing many and making them uncertain of the truth.

Job 31:33 — out of human weakness

St. Michael the Archangel

EVIL TRIES to confuse. Evil tries to create doubt. Evil tries to cloud what mankind is given from God. So take care always by focusing on God, on His love for mankind and the love He gives mankind in the sacraments. Then it will be much more difficult for evil to succeed.

Corruption

Jesus

WHEREVER EVIL is it corrupts and to look at mankind's history clearly shows this time and again.

Mother Mary

THE CORRUPTION in the world shows how much evil has seduced mankind.

THE CORRUPTION of evil in the world touches everyone but its effects can be minimized by each person if they reject what is wrong and embrace the right of my Son, Jesus.

Deceptions

Jesus

WHILE EVIL may appear to do good at times any good done is to cover up evil's true intentions and evil's actions. No lasting true good comes from evil.

THERE ARE those who even when shown the truth will refuse to believe it and prefer to believe in deceit and evil.

IT SHOULD not be surprising that anything that is evil is confusing because in evil nothing is clear as all is hidden in deception.

NO MATTER how it may appear evil can never bring true and lasting joy.

ANY OTHER spirit called on other than My Holy Spirit is a spirit of deceit and a spirit of evil which will bring confusion and suffering into lives, not healing.

God the Father

TO TRUST in evil is foolish as evil always deceives and always seeks to hurt mankind.

EVIL USES what appears attractive to promote its wrongs so as to touch and influence as many as possible.

DECEIT IS a weapon of evil so under no circumstance ever embrace it.

EVIL MANIPULATES the truth to suit itself.

HOW TRUE is the reward of heaven that awaits those who have lived in My love. How deceitful is the reward of evil that awaits those who have lived a life loving to sin.

Isaiah 40:10 — Here is his reward.

Mother Mary

SADLY LIES and deceit are so commonplace in the world today that at times it is hard to find the truth and because of this it is easier for evil to take souls into eternal darkness.

Defeated

Jesus

IN ME is the victory over evil, yet so many of My followers act as if they are the defeated.

Colossians 1:13 — He delivered us from the power of darkness.

EVIL ALWAYS tries to suppress love because it hates true love and it knows in true love it was defeated.

EVIL NEEDS to be confronted with true love for it is only in true love evil is defeated. I AM true love and in Me is the victory over evil to be found.

EVIL IS defeated but sadly many keep it alive and flourishing in the world by their immoral lives.

EVIL IS defeated, never doubt in My victory, even when it seems as if evil has won as this is only a deception of evil.

Mother Mary

EVIL IS at work always but in the lives of those who love my Son, Jesus, evil is always defeated.

Denial of God

St. James the Lesser

> GOD'S LOVE cannot be destroyed by evil or by man. It can only be denied and that denial brings a high cost to all who do so, angel or man.

Denying Good

Jesus

> ALL PEOPLE have within them goodness it is just that some deny this goodness and accept evil into their lives instead.
>
> EVIL WILL continue its wickedness as long as mankind allows it to by accepting sin and by doing what is wrong.

Destruction

God the Father

> I CREATED everything in love and it is in My love that creation is held together. That is why the evil one tries to destroy love as in doing so he hopes to unravel and destroy all I have created.
>
> EVIL WILL never stop trying to destroy mankind and I will never stop protecting mankind from evil. However, mankind also needs to protect itself by accepting My love and My help.

Jesus

EVIL TRIES to destroy mankind and in its foolish acceptance of sin mankind helps evil in its task.

EVIL MOCKS that which is good because it hates good and so wants to belittle or destroy good and uses mockery and falsehoods to do so.

GREED IS a cancer of evil that not only destroys lives but also destroys souls.

Mother Mary

EVIL HAS the desire to destroy mankind and has clearly shown this desire throughout history. Yet mankind foolishly ignores this truth and keeps embracing the deceits of that which desires its destruction.

EVIL DESTROYS yet many embrace it. God heals and loves yet many reject Him. True foolishness!

Distractions

St. Teresa of Avila

EVIL WILL try to distract you but if you pray for the grace to ignore evil and look beyond it God will give you that grace.

THOSE WHO seek to come closer to God will find many distractions along the path they walk. When you first start the journey so many hurdles can seem to be blocking the path but with faith and trust in God they can be overcome. However, it does not end there it just changes for as your spirit begins to grow in God's love so will the tricks that satan uses to distract you grow. When fear does not work, he will try seduction. When that fails, pride. When that fails, wealth and fame. When that fails, family and friends. When that fails he will abuse you during the spiritual moments to make you feel weak, unworthy, unloved.

At times the evil one will use a combination of all these. Then if he has not succeeded he may give you a rest so that you begin to think that you have defeated him. If you fall into that trap then the evil one uses subtle techniques to draw you into thoughts of how good you are to have beaten him. Then in many other ways he massages your ego so that now you may think more of yourself than God. It is very important that all people be on guard against evil's cunning and understand the evil one never gives up. Once you recognize this you will also see that in yourself you do not have the power to stand against the evil one but that when you are in God the evil one does not have the power to stand against you. It is when you see this that the path you walk becomes clearer and the spirituality you seek becomes deeper. However, the battle will become fiercer and the attacks will not stop. So, remember always, to place yourself in God's hands knowing that there you are secure and knowing in Him victory is assured.

Romans 8:26 — The spirit come to the aid of our weakness.

Drugs

God the Father

ADDICTIVE DRUGS are instruments that evil uses to draw people into the dark and to destroy their lives.

TO LEGALIZE drugs of addiction for pleasure does not make it right to use these instruments of evil, it only gives evil some larger acceptance by those in society.

Easter

Jesus

THE VICTORY is complete and evil knows defeat. The doors of heaven are opened wide and all who love Me are welcome inside. The eternal life in My glorious love awaits all who will through Me enter the heavenly gates.

IN MY death and resurrection the defeat of evil was complete, sadly though many desire to live in that defeat oblivious to what it will cost them in eternity. That cost is the highest price anyone could pay for it is their soul.

WITH MY defeat of evil came the opportunity for every person to be part of My victory if they so desire. They only have to truly choose to be part of it in Me.

THE ONLY ones to be turned away are those who reject My divine and victorious Easter day and those who embrace the evil one denying Me as God's only Son.

EVIL, THROUGH foolish people, will continue to try and deny My resurrection and My divinity. So do not be surprised by the frequent attacks on Me and on your faith in Me. Instead of worrying over them go out and boldly declare the truth of My resurrection, My divinity and My eternal loving victory over evil to all.

Mother Mary

MY SON, Jesus is risen from the dead victorious over evil bringing creation back into the love of God and opening the door to heaven to all of mankind who truly desire and seek it.

St. Peter the Apostle   Easter Sunday

CELEBRATE JOYFULLY today The Lord's victory. Celebrate joyfully today The Lord's defeat of evil. Celebrate joyfully today The Lord's undying love that defeated evil and offers all who will believe the opportunity to be part of His victory.

Psalm 97:1 — let the earth rejoice.

Empires

Jesus

THE ROMAN empire could not stand against My love, it fell before it as My chosen ones stood firm in My love. The Russian communist empire could not defeat My love, it collapsed as My chosen ones stood before it.

The sinful empire that exists today, like all the other empires that have opposed My love, will be defeated and fall before My chosen ones as they celebrate My victory over evil.

Zechariah 10:12 — and they shall walk in his name.

Eternity

God the Father

HELL HAS no end for those who are truly evil.

EVIL MAY have its day but I have eternity.

Jesus

THE EVIL mankind does is felt throughout eternity.

Equality

God the Father

REMEMBER ALL are equal in My eyes, it is only worldly eyes that see and create inequality under the influence of evil.

Families

Mother Mary

FAMILIES ARE meant to be full of happiness and love but sadly today many are not. The reason for this is because evil has entered the world and through the world attacks families in the hope of destroying society. In many ways evil is successful as it draws people into sin and selfishness turning them away from God. Without God's love in a family the family is bound to fail and today that is why so many do.

A SOUL is a gift of God to be treasured. Even the evil one treasures them while sadly many people do not.

False Humour

Jesus

THOSE WHO laugh at evil's false humour of sin open themselves to evil whose only intention is to have them crying in agony for eternity.

Fear

God the Father

IT IS through fear evil causes many to sin. It is in trust that many overcome sin and find security in Me.

Sirach 2:13 — Woe to the faint of heart who trust not.

When a person lets fear into their heart they open a way for evil to attack them and weaken the trust the person may have in Me. In this life there is nothing to fear. If a person loves Me and believes I will take care of them then in the next life there will be eternal joy to look forward to in My love.

Jesus

Have no fear of evil, let evil fear your trust in Me.

To fear evil is what evil wants people to do as fear is a weapon evil uses to draw people away from Me and into sin. Never fear evil and always let evil fear you by living in complete trust in My love for you and the victory of My love over evil.

In fear evil thrives, in trust of Me evil dies.

Fear no evil instead let evil fear you as you live for Me, in Me and with Me.

It is only those who reject My love and embrace the hatred of evil that need fear judgement day.

Why fear evil, for it is defeated. Why fear what evil may do to you in this life, for if you hold onto My love any suffering in this life will lead to glory in heaven. Why fear evil in your life, for in Me your life is safe.

Psalm 107:6 — The Lord who rescued them.

Holy Spirit

To fear evil is to leave a door open to it.

Mother Mary

WITH TRUST in God there should be no concern over the future or no fear of evil.

THE FEAR of death is a fruit of the evil one who works hard to make people not believe in the life to come. So that in this life people seek as much pleasure as possible and believe there is no price to pay for their sins. Then death is seen as the end and not as the doorway to eternal life as it is meant to be and it is this that brings fear.

HAVE NO fright, have no terror, have no fear of evil for if you keep your love of My Son, Jesus, in the Eucharist, it is evil that is frightened of you.

DO NOT be afraid of evil, stand tall in my Son, Jesus', love against it and know that in eternity you are victorious against evil.

St. Benedict

THERE IS nothing to fear in the love of Jesus. There is nothing to fear in a life given to Jesus. There is nothing to fear in a complete giving of self to Jesus, for His love will surround you and protect you from all that is evil.

THE WORST evil can do to you it can only do if you allow it by your fears, uncertainties and doubts. Holding firm to Jesus evil can do you no everlasting harm.

Isaiah 12:2 — God indeed is my saviour; I am confident and unafraid.

St. Aloyisius

IT IS in fear evil thrives. It is in trust your love of God will overcome evil.

St. Blaise

MANY PEOPLE want to declare their love for God but because of their fears of what the world may say about them or do to them remain silent. It is this silence that allows evil to spread in the world for those who support sin are very loud in their promotion of it. If those who love God ignore their fears and trust that God will see them through any adversity, then speak loudly and lovingly of His love in their lives, the holy chorus they would create would break the grasp of evil on the world.

Psalm 57:10 — I will praise you among the peoples Lord, I will chant your praise among the nations.

St. Andrew

EVIL COWERS in the presence of God so if you try to live every moment in God's presence evil will cower at you.

Fighting Evil

God the Father

FIGHT EVIL only with true love as this is the only way to overcome it. My Son, Jesus, is true love so fight evil in, with, and through Him.

THERE IS a battle taking place in every life in every moment and it is the battle for the soul. No one should doubt this is happening as it is in disbelief a person stops fighting and risks losing their soul in the battle to evil.

Mother Mary

THE MORE you do for God the less influence evil has. The more you do for God the less damage evil can do. The more you do for God the less harm evil can inflict upon the world.

Jeremiah 15:21 — free you from the hand of the wicked.

St. Michael Archangel

THE BATTLE between good and evil goes on in every moment but in the lives of those who love God the victory of Christ, Our Lord, over evil is seen in every moment.

IN THE battle between good and evil there is no place for apathy or indifference as they only place a person in the hands of evil. Everyone needs to be actively fighting against evil if they want to secure a place in heaven for themselves and for others.

IN THE war of good against evil you will only win if you fight with love. Fighting any other way may at times seem like a victory but in the end you will find it is a defeat where you were led into sin, which is just what evil wants and which is a victory for evil.

Psalm 1:6 — the way of the wicked leads to ruin.

AS MANY people discover, the fight against evil is long and hard, but it is a fight that people can win by totally embracing the love of God in Jesus, His only Son. It is in the true love of God the deceit of evil can be overcome as the strength of His love gives people, by His Holy Spirit, the power to defeat evil.

Foolish

Jesus

EVIL MAKES fools of sinners.

EVIL TRIES to make good look foolish by blinding mankind to the foolishness of evil. It is foolish to bargain with evil as evil will never keep its promises, for this goes against the very nature of evil.

MANY PEOPLE foolishly let evil blind them to the true cost of sin but this will not stop them having to pay that price which may be very high indeed.

THE CORRUPTION in the world is far greater than anyone knows. However, evil knows and is happy at mankind's foolishness and weakness.

THE SERPENT of evil still tries to seduce people into his nest of suffering and foolishly many people embrace freely his seduction.

EVIL WISHES no one to have good lives and does what it can to make it so. Foolishly many do not believe this and ignore this fact at their peril.

IT IS unwise to watch evil happening and say nothing about it. For by your silence you then allow evil to grow.

Wisdom 12:2 — Warn them, and remind them of the sins they are committing.

A WISE person avoids evil at all costs, even the smallest evil. Evil desires to destroy mankind. I desire to bring mankind to eternal joy. The choice is mankind's and it should choose wisely.

TRUE VALUES are distorted by evil and, foolishly by mankind, under evil's influence so that the values many embrace are false and the ones rejected by many are often true.
This is the way of evil making what is true seem wrong and what is false seem right. Foolishly, so many people are blind to this in their pride and in their apathy.

MONEY BECOMES everything to those who truly know nothing about life and what it is. Blinded by money eternity is obscured and all focus is placed on life on earth and the pleasures that can be had in it. The value of eternal life is ignored, dismissed or rejected as irrelevant. Foolishly, people who live this way will have to pay a far higher price than any wealth they have on earth. In eternity they will regret placing so much value on that which in eternity is of no value. Sadly, so many will come to know the truth too late and will spend eternity reflecting on their foolishness and paying the price that is demanded of them from evil.

ONLY THE foolish believe evil will give them what they need in life as it will only bring them what is empty and what leads to death and the suffering of the soul.

Holy Spirit

IT IS foolish to trust in that which cannot be trusted. Sadly today so many do, as they trust in the evil in the world, hoping their so-called rights, which often are truly wrongs, to bring a better future.

Mother Mary

MY CHILDREN on earth can live happy lives if they choose to but unfortunately they keep choosing sadness as my children keep choosing bad over good, suffering over peace, the world over heaven, and the evil one over God. What foolishness!

EVIL LAUGHS at mankind's foolishness as people embrace evil's ways for the evil one knows that mankind will only suffer from doing so. Sadly many people do not know this or many do not believe this and that is truly foolish.

Force

Jesus

TO FORCE your will upon others is to do as evil does and not to do as I do for I never force My will on anyone.

VIOLENCE IS a weapon of evil not of God.

Mother Mary

THOSE WHO use violence to achieve their goals may find in eternity the violence of evil as their reward for their actions on earth.

Freedom

Jesus

NO ONE should be left alone to sink into the quagmire of sin and all who love Me should be helping the sinners break free from the evil that ensnares them.

A MAN one day looked at the world around him and wondered why it was in such a mess. All he could see was turmoil; everywhere there seemed to be death and destruction, selfishness and greed, evil, immorality and lustfulness. Yet he saw so little true happiness. "Surely," he thought, "this is wrong, surely life is meant to be better than this?" He then realized that he was part of the problem because he had accepted many of these things into his life. He looked at his own life and saw that he too had little true happiness. He saw that his life was one full of stress as he tried to live the way of the world. "If I continue to live this way then the future looks bleak. Do I want to carry on with this pointless life where I worry, I am stressed, I am working long hours and all I have to show for this are a few worldly things? Yes, I have a house, a nice car, and plenty of money but what use are these, they do not comfort my heart and bring peace to my soul. Shall I keep seeking the goods and pleasures of the world and remain empty within and when I die these things are no use to me, I cannot take them with me."

As he considered these insights it became clear that he should change his life. The man started to see that if he did not change himself first how could the world be expected to change. Inside grew the knowledge that he must do something, not only for himself, for the whole of mankind. As he saw in many people he knew, living similar lives to him, having the same blindness and the same unhappiness, he wanted to help them find a better life too.

"I must change and I must be an example to others so that they desire to change also," he said to himself with a determination unknown to him before. "That's it!" he thought as a revelation came upon him. "If I want the world to be better I first must be and I must, by the example of my life, help others to be better too." Inside for the first time in his life there was a certainty that this was the right thing to do. There was a peace he had never known before and yes, a joyful excitement. "Why do I feel so good?" he wondered. Then he thought he heard a voice in his head say, "Because you have discovered the truth and the truth sets you free."

"I am free!" he said out loud realizing that no longer did he feel stressed or worried over anything. Seeing now that as he decided to turn from the ways of the world and the ways of evil in the world to a better way it was as if chains had fallen from him and truly he was set free. "How shall I start my new life?" he mused, when that same voice replied, gently, "In Me."

"Who are You?" asked the man, surprised he would speak to a voice in his head.

"I am the truth that has set you free, that will lead you to a true and full life; a better life in Me."

The man fell to his knees and cried out loud, "Lord," as he realized it was Jesus speaking to him.

"Take My holy word into your heart and live to it from now on and you will find the life you seek," replied the voice.

Before him now, in his mind's eye the man saw the Holy Bible. "Of course, of course," he said with a smile. "I ignored it before, how foolish I was for all the answers are here," he stated, shaking his head as he thought what a fool he had been ignoring God's Word and listening to the world's word instead. "What had that brought me?" he thought. "Very little indeed and what does that bring society? Very little good and lots of confusion, uncertainty, turmoil, suffering, disrespect, immorality and hatred as mankind follows the guidance of evil instead of that of God. Now is the time to change. Now, not later. Now I will no longer be foolish. Now I will be true to God, to myself and to mankind as I am supposed to be."

The man felt renewed within and decided from now on he would serve God and serve fellow man. He would become a servant to all, serving them the help, guidance and love they needed to overcome evil in their lives wherever he could. Then he heard a voice in his head say, "That is what you are supposed to do, for you are a Christian and that is the Christian way."

Today many of My followers have forgotten this. It is time, like this man, they remembered.

THE TRUTH sets people free of the shackles of evil's deceits.

EVIL CANNOT imprison those who truly love Me.

THE TRUTH frees people as evil cannot hold those who live in the truth of My love.

God the Father

TRUE FREEDOM is a right I gave to all mankind and one that evil in many forms tries to take away by enslaving people through pride and sin.

Gentleness

Jesus

THERE ARE many evil foxes in the world today looking to trap and devour the gentle lambs of My love. However, it is in the gentleness of My love that My lambs will be secure and need fear none for I shall protect them and no evil or cunning can stand against Me.

Ezekiel 31:14 — all of them are destined for death for the land below.

GENTLENESS WINS the hearts of all who are not full of evil and it can even win the hearts of many of those full of evil.

Goodness

God the Father

UNLESS YOU respond to evil with goodness evil will grow.

MY NEWS is always good it is only evil that brings bad news.

THE GOOD in the world may be hidden by the bad but it is still there working strongly against evil.

GOODNESS ABOUNDS in the world even though it may not seem so. Many people are trying to live good lives and to do what is right but so often this is not heard of. Instead, it is the bad and evil in the world that makes the news and because of this many despair thinking there is no or little good happening.

Jesus

TO DO the best in any situation is always to do good, not evil.

THERE IS plenty of good news happening around the world but people seem more fascinated by the bad news because the good has been devalued by the evil in society.

Mother Mary

WHEN OTHERS behave badly, respond in goodness and love, otherwise evil wins.

NO GOOD ever comes from evil or what is bad even though at times it may seem as if it does. All good comes from the goodness of God's love not from the darkness of evil.

WITH GOOD intentions, good actions and a good heart all that will come from a person is goodness and no evil at all.

GOODNESS ALWAYS wins in the end even though at the time people may not see or understand this. Good always defeats evil, this is an eternal truth that cannot be changed.

Hatred

God the Father

THE HATRED in the world shows how strong is the grip of evil.

Jesus

IN THE love of Me no one hates and in the love of evil no one loves.

Hell

God the Father

HELL IS not on earth and cannot be experienced on earth. Hell is beyond the understanding of mankind but sadly is not beyond the reach of those who do evil and sin.

Justifying Evil

God the Father

SIN DESTROYS lives and wounds souls even when the sin seems so insignificant it still has these effects as that is what evil does through sin.
Even though at times because of acts of evil My goodness reaches out to touch lives this does not mean I condone evil as I never do. Always it would have been better if the evil had never happened regardless of what good results may have come. I just use the situation to bring good but never do I desire, support or endorse any act of evil.

Jesus

USING EVIL to achieve good never succeeds. Yet, many believe it can and find justifications for doing so; justifications that are only excuses for accepting evil and that will return to torment those who use evil for any reason.

Keeping Evil at Bay

God the Father

ALWAYS BE prepared to face evil and never be afraid of doing so.

MY LOVE is a barrier against evil and when you live and serve in My love you are safe.

Mother Mary

NO MATTER how the evil one tries he cannot overcome a person who truly loves God and completely trusts in Him.

THE LOSS of a soul to evil is a tragedy that can always be avoided if only the person seeks true forgiveness in my Son Jesus' merciful love.

Jesus

THE SACRAMENTS keep you in My love. The sacraments strengthen you in My love. The sacraments keep evil at bay by filling you with My love, strengthening your faith and giving you the courage that is needed to stand firm in My truth.

2 Corintians 7:4 — filled with...
Ephesians 6:20 — the courage to speak...
Isaiah 34:16 — of the lord...
1 Timothy 1:5 — and a sincere faith.

ONLY WITH true love can evil be defeated in a person's life. I AM true love and in My love is the victory over evil that all can be part of.

FACE EVIL with My love, with My goodness, and with My truth, and then evil cannot overcome you.

AS A person tries to live to My way evil tries hard to stop them but if they persevere in love of Me evil cannot overcome them.

Led by Evil

God the Father

EVIL LEADS people into accepting what is foolish and what is stupid as being what is right and what is best for society.

Jesus

DO NOT let evil lead you into anger and resentment. Forgive and love and stay on My path.

HAVE THE love of Me and have the love of others on your heart at all times and you will not be led astray by evil.

TO THINK badly of anyone is to let evil into your thoughts.

Mother Mary

DO NOT let the evil one lead you into bad thoughts of others. Try always to think the best of and for others.

Life

God the Father

> THERE ARE many theories on the formation of life but only one is true and that is all life came from Me through My Son, Jesus, and by the power of My Holy Spirit. There are many theories on the creation of man but only one is true and that is I created man in My image and breathed My living spirit into his being to create his soul. There are many theories on how life has evolved but only the one that says all life came from God and lives in God's love by God's will is true. All else are deceptions of evil used to devalue the wonderful gift I have given in mankind.
>
> *Psalm 55:11 — Within are mischief and evil.*

MY WILL is that life is treasured and respected. Evil's will is that life is destroyed.

HOW EVIL laughs at the way mankind places little value on life as evil knows I place great value on life. Evil is pleased that mankind offends Me in the devaluing of this great gift of My love.

Jesus

> TO GIVE life little value is to devalue oneself and is to do just as evil desires.

Living in God

God the Father

IF A person lives away from Me they live the way that leads to hell. If a person lives to My way then they live away from evil and live the way that leads to heaven. If a person lives to My way they live to the way of My Son, Jesus. In Him is the only way to live in heaven eternally.

I CREATED in love and if mankind lived as it was created to live then love would be in all it does and evil would be unable to cause chaos on earth.

LIFE ON earth is part of the total life of a person, not the complete life. After passing through the doorway of death, eternity awaits in heaven for those who in their life on earth have done their best to live as I asked. Purgatory awaits for those who have made mistakes that need to be atoned for before they can be welcomed into heaven. Hell awaits those who have denied My love and turned from Me deep into a life of sin and evil. It is important that people understand what this life on earth leads to. Important so they can make the right decisions that will bring them to live in My love forever.

Sirach 15:16 — Whichever you choose.

Jesus

EVIL CAN never overcome a person who loves and lives for My presence in the Eucharist.

EVIL CAN never overcome a person who truly lives for Me. This is an eternal truth that no one should doubt.

Loving Hearts

God the Father

A HEART begins to close to Me when it focuses on self and when it allows self to lead it into sin. As a heart closes to Me it begins to wither and will eventually die because it no longer has My love residing in it and My love is the food of life for hearts. A heart in its death throes often calls out in anger, bitterness, hatred, resentment and in many other evil ways as it attempts to hurt others because it is hurting and wants others to be the same way. These hearts are to be pitied. These hearts are hearts I still love and do not want to lose. It is important that when those who do love Me come in contact with these bitter hearts they do not allow this infection of evil to spread into their hearts. Sometimes the loving hearts can be hurt and in their pain allow their weaknesses to take hold and it is then through these weaknesses the infection of evil can enter. The hearts that love Me must strengthen themselves in grace through the sacraments and prayer, so that when they come in contact with a dying heart the good hearts can stand firm in My love, and reach out in My love to the bitter hearts in the hope of saving them from the evil that has been let in. The dying hearts need healing and this can only happen by the graces I grant through the hearts of those that love and serve Me. I call to each person who professes to love Me to become My loving heart on earth and take My healing love to those who are dying in evil. Do it by placing your heart into the Sacred Heart of My Son, Jesus, and by asking the Immaculate Heart of Mary His mother to help you.

St. Michael the Archangel

NO EVIL can penetrate a heart that truly loves God.

Marriage

Jesus

LOVE BETWEEN a husband and wife is meant to be sacred and is meant to grow in Me so as to strengthen society and the world. That is why marriage is under intense attack from evil as the evil one wants to prevent the true love in marriages from blessing the world.

Mother Mary

A RELATIONSHIP between a man and a woman in the sacrament of marriage is sacred. Any who destroy or attack this sacred gift, attack the God-given sanctity and will have to answer for that.
A relationship between a man and a woman is the relationship God created to be. Any relationship of the same sex, be it male or female, is a terrible sin against God the creator. A sin that will lead many into despair when they meet God on judgement day and come to know the truth and know they lived far from it. A relationship between a man and a woman should be built on love and mutual respect. Any who do not respect the love of a marriage build a cross for themselves and those within their family. Relationships between men and women are an important part of God's plan of creation and so they should be respected, filled with love and be in line with the commandments God has given otherwise relationships only become ways to relate to evil and sin and ways to take people away from God.

Malachi 3:22 — Remember the law.
Proverbs 15:16 — Of The Lord.

Negotiating with Evil

Jesus

IT IS impossible to negotiate a successful and good outcome with evil as evil never keeps its word and would never do anything that is good and has good fruits.

New Age

Jesus

THERE ARE many new so-called beliefs put to mankind today. Beliefs which are there to lead mankind away from Me. These beliefs are not new at all but old deceptions presented in a new way. They are the same deceptions that evil has been using since mankind was first created. Now, as in the past, mankind is blind to what is really put before it and now, as before, many are drawn into the lies of evil that snares their very souls and in the end will destroy them.

Jeremiah 23:32 — They do this people no good at all.

Offending God

Jesus

A PRECIOUS gift from God. A treasure from heaven. A creation of love. That is a soul and it is no wonder evil tries to destroy as many as possible for each soul evil takes it sees as a way of hurting God. A way that evil thinks will bring victory. How sad evil has not yet accepted its defeat and how sad so many souls on earth do not believe in it either.

Proverbs 11:19 — he who pursues evil does so to his death.

WHEN MANKIND compares itself to the animals and believes it comes from them it lowers the dignity of mankind and reduces the magnificent truth of God's love in His children. This is but a deception of evil that many are drawn into. This is a way that evil tries to demean mankind. As people lose their belief in the special creation of love from the Father that mankind is, they deny the truth of God's word. For it is in that word God gave mankind a spirit in the image of Himself, a spirit which no animal has. Not only does evil trick people into offending God in this way but also offends God by saying that I, His Son, Jesus, came into the body of an animal that just evolved in a different way than other animals. How offensive this is for it is an insult not only to humanity but also to divinity. Evil is deceiving mankind into denying its own worth and into denying that God came to earth in a creation that is above others and created to be an image of God's love. Once again evil attacks God through mankind's weakness of pride and leads mankind into a lowering of its worth. No wonder it becomes easier to destroy human life or to alter its structure for when it is seen as little more than an animal then it is harder to see the wrong that is done.

Genesis 1:27 — God created man in his image, in the divine image he created him; male and female he created them.

Open to Evil

God the Father

WHEN LOVE leaves a heart evil enters it.

THE MORE you focus on evil the more you risk it coming into your life.

Jesus

TO HOLD resentment in your heart is to hold a door open to evil.

NO ONE needs evil in their lives but sadly many believe they do and by the way they live it is clear to see that many freely invite and embrace evil into their lives.

UNDER NO circumstance put the way of the world before My way for if you do you risk opening yourself to evil.

THE WORLD is open to evil because mankind chooses for it to be so.

NO ONE should turn to evil for any reason as the price for doing so is always very high.

TO SUPPORT evil is to support one's own destruction.

HAVE NO acceptance of sin on your heart and have no way for evil to enter it.

Mother Mary

THERE IS a daily battle with evil in all lives. Unfortunately many lose that battle and succumb to evil because many no longer have the protection of God's grace by their acceptance of that which opposes and denies God's will.

DO NOT let evil draw you into thinking badly of others or saying bad things about them as in this way evil enters your heart.

IF YOU look to evil you invite evil into your life. Always look to heaven and only invite God into your life if you desire to be safe eternally.

THE ENTRY of evil into mankind's hearts was caused by pride and can be ended by true humility before God.

NEVER ACCEPT sin in any form as in doing so you invite evil into your life.

St. John the Baptist

TO PROTEST against God's will is to embrace the evil one who does the same.

Peace

God the Father

> PEACE REIGNS supreme in hearts where My Son, Jesus is Lord, for He is peace.
> Peace reigns supreme in lives where My Son, Jesus is Lord, for with Jesus in a person's life nothing really disturbs the person's peace.
> Peace reigns supreme in souls where My Son, Jesus is Lord, for then no evil can reside there and without evil there is always peace.
>
> *Jeremiah 34:5 — In peace.*

Jesus

> I BRING peace – the evil one brings turmoil.
>
> PEACE SHOULD be the desire of all people but foolishly, because some do not desire peace, turmoil is widespread in the world and evil reigns in many hearts taking them into eternal agony.

Pleasure

Jesus

> THOSE WHO find pleasure in evil will discover that it is a false pleasure that leads to eternal displeasure.
>
> EVIL IN entertainment makes the entertainment sinful.

WHILE EVIL may seem exciting and glamorous all should remember the price evil demands for its false pleasures and that is misery and suffering eternally.

Politics

God the Father

EVIL MANIPULATES politicians to do its will knowing that by doing so it can get many more to accept its will. Pray for all politicians to have the strength of heart to resist evil and do only what is good.

Jesus

SADLY, POLITICS leads some people to deceive as they seek power or seek to keep power. Because of this a doorway is open to the evil one who enters and manipulates many politicians to do, support, or accept wrong.

WHEN DEMOCRACY rules, unless it is a democracy that follows My way, it will be a democracy that leads to turmoil, confusion, suffering and eventually into the arms of evil. Democracy is not the way of salvation and peace for mankind. I AM and My way is.

St. John the Baptist

DEMOCRACY ONLY works for the best if the majority have good intentions that avoid sin, reject evil, and promote what is right.

Prayer

God the Father

As PRAYER grows in the world evil reduces.

Mother Mary

WHEN EVIL tries to distract you from your prayers ignore it by focusing on the love in your heart for God and let this love draw you closer to the love of God as your heart then opens to receive His grace within.

Pride

Jesus

LIFE FOR mankind today is the same as life for mankind throughout its existence. It is a life of choices between good and evil. Today, sadly, as before, many choose evil and choose to embrace all that comes with evil and just as before in their blind pride many do not see this or believe it.

EVIL IS infectious because many souls have the open wound of pride that allows evil in.

NEVER IN pride look down on others as doing so will open you to evil.

IT IS because of the pride and decadence of mankind that evil is strong in the world.

It is pride that makes a person consider any other person inferior. The same pride that lucifer and the evil angels have as they consider mankind inferior.

It is important always to treat people with the same respect you expect for yourself, not to do so is prideful and opens you to evil.

Pride draws people away from God into the arms of the evil one and blinds them to what they are doing.

Priesthood

God the Father

Every priest deserves respect for the sacrifices they have made to become a priest. Every priest deserves understanding for the struggles they face and the weaknesses they have. Every priest deserves help in fighting their battles in the priestly life.
Never let a priest stand alone. Always help priests with your prayers and support, understanding evil never stops attacking the priestly life. Always respect the work priests do for it is holy even if at times the priest is not.

Jesus

When a priest falls it is a disaster for the whole world as it lets evil's grasp become firmer on mankind.

Mother Mary

> IN THE heart of a priest is the grace to overcome all evil and for this grace to do so the priest only needs to believe and to use this grace.

Recognizing Evil

God the Father

> EVIL TAKES many forms and it is only in obedience to My commandments, the word of My Son, Jesus, and the teachings of My Holy, Catholic and Apostolic Church that a person can recognize evil in all its forms.

Selfishness

Jesus

> TO THINK of self first is to put the needs of others second and this is not what I ask of My followers. I ask you to put the love of God first and others to be treated in the same way you would want to be treated yourself. Anything other than this goes against My command and leads only into sin and evil.
>
> *Amos 9:9 — I have given the command.*

Sexual Relationships

Jesus

LUST REPLACES love and society suffers as families fall apart; the young become confused and evil laughs. Without love there is no hope for the future, with lust there is only disaster.

Baruch 1:6 — flushed with shame.

ANY SEX outside of marriage is unsafe as it opens the people involved to the seductions of evil and that is not safe.

SO OFTEN people within the church see with their human eyes and see what they want, not what I want. Contraception for many Christians is seen as a personal choice but the only personal choice in this is whether or not the person will sin. The interference with the formation of life with any form of contraception is wrong. The only choice that is sin free is to abstain at the times when life may be formed, for in abstaining nothing is done that affects the life that may be created, nothing is done to block the formation of life, and nothing is done to debase the gift of life the Father may give. Abstinence is the only way that does not offend God while contraception is the way that offends not only God but the souls it prevents from having life on earth. Contraception is an evil which not only debases life but also brings many to insult the gift God has given them in their bodies. A gift which many souls are denied because of the selfishness of those who think of themselves and forget the will of God. Contraception is a grievous sin which many are blinded to and which many will have to answer for on their last day.

Ecclesiasticus 2:21 — This also is vanity and a great misfortune.
Micah 3:4 — Rather shall he hide his face from them at that time, because of the evil they have done.

Sex is a gift to be treasured and respected between a husband and a wife. Remember same sex marriage is same sex sin. Unfortunately, for many people sex has become just another physical act with no love and no true appreciation of the gift. How the evil one smiles seeing how easy it is to draw people into immorality and through this how marriages, families and societies can be damaged grievously.

Mother Mary

Sexual union is meant to be a sacred and loving part of a marriage so that the love in a marriage can be strengthened and so children can be born. Today the true meaning of sex has been hidden by the evil one as he draws many into lustful and immoral ways which weaken the sanctity of marriage and in so doing help weaken and destroy society. Sadly, many are blind to this evil because of their prideful, selfish pleasure-seeking ways and cannot see that they hold some responsibility for the woes of the world because of their sinful ways.

St. Columban

In the world today many live by few morals and accept immorality as the norm. Those who do so place their very souls at risk of eternal damnation. It is the duty of everyone who claims to love Jesus, Our Lord, to stand and proclaim the truth. To tell in love their brothers and sisters how the immorality they live by is wrong and is from evil. To explain to their brothers and sisters that unless lives are changed to good and moral ones, suffering and pain will continue to grow in the world and that for many of the immoral it will continue into eternity.

Luke 3:3 — proclaiming a baptism of repentance.

Suffering

God the Father

UNDER THE influence of evil many hurt themselves and others either physically or emotionally and always spiritually. Yet many do not recognize what they do and the consequences of it and often foolishly believe there is no price to pay for doing wrong. Always there is a price and always that price is painful and sometimes that pain can be eternal.

IT IS always the innocent who suffer the most from evil because evil targets the innocents as it sees in them a way of hurting mankind deeply with the hope of making the innocent change to become the guilty so as to perpetuate the pain.

MANKIND FOOLISHLY walks the path of self destruction guided by evil along this path. Due to this mankind brings upon itself unnecessary suffering and brings to the evil one in its suffering great pleasure. In its pride mankind rejects the path of peace, love and joy I offer in My Son, Jesus, and pays a high price for doing so. I still offer and I still wait for mankind to accept My offer and to reject the unnecessary pain it now embraces in accepting the ways of the evil one.

NO ONE should suffer for expressing their faith in Me but sadly many do because evil tries to destroy that faith and stop it spreading.

Jesus

EVIL KNOWS no boundaries to the suffering it causes, the more suffering the more evil is pleased, but it will never be satisfied until all suffer unceasingly in evil's grasp.

THE SUFFERING soul is one trapped by sin. An enslaved soul is one surrounded by evil. A lost soul is one that accepts the evil that surrounds it and falls into the trap of satan.

Amos 5:16 — *There shall be lamentation.*

AS THE world turns away from Me the evil one laughs as mankind invites the suffering he offers into the world.

St. Cornelius

TO SUFFER for The Lord Jesus is a grace-filled gift that can help so many walk past evil and into the arms of God. It is by the suffering of some for the love of God that others are graced to find that love. So every time you suffer offer it to The Lord Jesus for others and see by His grace many saved.

Psalm 112:7 — Their hearts are steadfast trusting in The Lord.
Philippians 3:10 — And sharing of his sufferings.

Superstitions

Jesus

IF, IN following Me, people bring old beliefs that are wrong, old superstitions and hold onto these as part of their faith then these people risk losing their faith and losing My love as all they do is hold Me with a similar respect to these old evils and that is a grave sin.

The taking of Life

God the Father

THE MARK of evil is upon many souls because of their support of abortion or their support of those who are pro abortion.

Jesus

THOSE WHO welcome the killing of others welcome evil into their lives; evil that they may have to endure eternally.

Temptations

God the Father

DO NOT be drawn into thoughts of self by the temptations evil puts before you. Always focus on how My Son, Jesus, served others and put others before Himself, then try your best to do the same, not forgetting to pray for the grace to do so.

Jesus

WHEN THE temptations of evil come do not focus on them. Try to look beyond them and focus on My love for it is in My love you will find the strength to resist all temptation.

THE TEMPTATIONS of evil are not always obvious so pray for the grace to see them for what they are.

IT TAKES a disciplined heart to follow Me and not to be drawn into the temptations of evil; a heart disciplined by love.

Terrorism

God the Father

NO ONE who sows terror in My name does My will or pleases Me as they do the will of the evil one who is truly pleased with them.

Jesus

TERRORISTS PLEASE the evil one not God. No matter what the cause terrorism is never good and can never be truly justified.

St. Teresa of Avila

THROUGHOUT HISTORY people have been killing each other and often for the smallest of reasons. Today there are many dealing in the evil of terror and killing whomsoever they can. These terrorists often believe they are freedom fighters but they do not understand there is no freedom in sin. Sometimes these confused people claim to be doing it for God or that it is God's will. How foolish they are to be deceived so easily by evil and how sorry they will be when they stand before God. These people should understand that God treasures life and abhors the taking of life no matter what the reason or what the belief. These sowers of terror should also understand, unless they repent and change their ways, that is they who will suffer eternally. To commit mortal sin for your country, your faith or in revenge will cost your soul and no country is worth that. Any faith that asks one to do so is not of God and any pleasure found in revenge will be short lived while the suffering will be eternal. Freedom only comes in God and if you break His command "Thou shalt not kill," and do it knowingly then you will find only slavery in hell awaiting. Come to your senses, those who kill, and seek God's forgiveness before it is too late.

Jeremiah 25:32 — Lo calamity stalks.

The Church

Jesus

> EVIL NEVER overcame Me and it will never overcome My One Holy, Catholic and Apostolic Church.

Mother Mary

> WHEN A person is obedient to God's will and to His Holy, Catholic and Apostolic Church then there is nothing evil can do to stop the person bringing souls to God.

> AS A person tries to live as my Son, Jesus asks the world will try to stop them because the evil one works through the world. However, if the person keeps close to my Son, Jesus, in the sacraments, in Holy Scripture, in prayer and in obedience to His One Holy, Catholic and Apostolic Church, the world will be unable to stop or imprison the person because the person will be free and unstoppable in my Son, Jesus' love and grace.

St. Agnes

> EVEN THOUGH mankind may sway in the wind of evil the church must remain solid in the love of God and in obedience to His commandments.

Philippians 1:27 — standing firm in one spirit with one mind struggling together for the faith of the gospel...
Philippians 1:28 — not intimidated in any way by your opponents.

St. Edmund

TODAY THE faith given by God Himself comes under attack from all sides but do not be afraid that the faith will fall. The universal faith of the One, Holy Catholic and Apostolic Church, the faith of the truth, cannot be overcome for it is full of God's power, a power none can defeat. The faithful today are called to stand in the truth Our Lord, Jesus, gave to us, believing in His victorious love, fearing no evil and carrying all the crosses He in His mercy may give to the faithful. Doing so, the faithful will bring glory to God and in that glory many souls of the lost will be touched and be brought to His glory also.

John 12:15 — fear no more
Isaiah 4:6 — for over all, his glory will be a shelter and protection.

The Face of Evil

Jesus

EVIL HAS many faces and each one of them is truly horrible even though at times they may not seem so.

Holy Spirit

EVIL COMES in many forms but none of them are for the benefit of mankind.

Mother Mary

IN THE face of evil always show love and you will always be victorious over it.

The Grasp of Evil

Jesus

>   Evil will use whatever means necessary to draw people into its grasp. That is why people must be careful in all they do not to accept even the smallest evil because then evil will have hold of them.
>
>   If there is no way to stop a people sinning, even though you have tried your hardest, then pray for them and pray for their souls not to be taken by evil.
>
>   Evil holds onto the world because mankind keeps inviting it to.
>
>   Until the world appreciates and accepts that God visited the world in His only Son and accept that The Father and I and The Holy Spirit are The One true God, evil will have a hold on the world.

Holy Spirit

>   Until the world embraces My love evil will have a hold on mankind.

Mother Mary

>   Do not let evil draw you into memories of sin as it is easy in those memories to be drawn into sinful thoughts and desires.
>
>   Evil drives people to madness, as anyone who embraces evil is truly not sane.

The Reign of Evil

God the Father

ON THIS hallowed eve (Halloween) evil may seem to reign in many celebrations but remember My love reigns above all eternally and not for one moment does evil overcome it. This is truly worth celebrating.

Jesus

IF EVIL seems to rule on earth remember it does not, and it never will, for it is My love that reigns supreme and always will.

EVIL MAY be prominent in the world and may hurt many people but remember My love is victorious over evil and it can heal all who are hurt by evil.

WHEN EVIL reigns in a person's heart not only do they suffer and all those around them but so does all of mankind as the evil affects the balance of good and evil in the world.

EVIL WILL come to an end but My love will not.

Mother Mary

GREED IS rampant in the world and because of this evil has free reign in many hearts.

EVIL REIGNS in the hearts of sinners who will not repent and will reign over them in eternity unless they change.

The Word of God

God the Father

AS PEOPLE read My words often they forget to meditate on the true meaning and just give a cursory glance to each word. How important it is that time is spent to think about what each sentence says and what it means in a person's life. People should ask My Holy Spirit to lead them to a deeper understanding of the words I give to mankind so that these words can come alive in their lives. My words are living words but people can become dead to them by not putting into action what I say. All that I give to mankind is goodness. All that I give to mankind is for their betterment. All that I give to mankind is given in love. Mankind needs to accept what I give in love and then to act in love on what I have given. So often people do not do this, so often they read, think they understand and do little or nothing of what I have asked. This is no understanding at all. Throughout the history of mankind I have given My guiding words but frequently mankind has not listened and the results are there for all to see. Pain, suffering, evil and sin abound in the world where instead there should be love, peace and hope. People need to listen to Me, their heavenly Father and to follow the advice I give to them, if they do so life will be good for that is how I created it to be. My words, My advice and My help are there for all people and for each person the message is the same. It is to love Me, your God above all others and to love one another as I have loved you through My Son, Jesus. It is a very clear directive and yet to many it seems to be hidden behind a cloud of pride and of self. Sometimes this cloud obscures the message completely and all that can be seen is a haze of sin and evil. Once again I say to My children on earth follow these words of love and live a good, a happy and a fulfilled life. Once again I say to My children on earth I love you and I want you with Me forever. Once again I say to My children on earth listen to your Father who created you and who knows what is best for you. Listen My children, listen!

Sirach 42:18 — Their innermost being he understands, the most high possesses all knowledge.

Tool of Evil

Jesus

JEALOUSY IS a vicious tool of evil, one that hurts not only the jealous one but others too. Evil does not admit its wrongs as it sees no need to and sees nothing to be repentant over in them. Jealousy opens a heart to evil.

True Power

God the Father

EVIL CANNOT overcome any who truly love Me for their love is insurmountable.

EVIL CANNOT ensnare those who truly love My Son, Jesus, as their love in His love is stronger than all evil.

THE POWER of My love sustains all of creation while the hate of evil starves creation of what it needs to exist.

Jesus

THE POWER of one drop of My blood is greater than that of all evil.

THE POWER of evil at times may seem so large but in comparison to the power of God it is nothing at all.

Philippians 3:21 — The power that enables him also to bring all things into subjection to himself.

TRUSTING IN Me makes you stronger than evil.

THE GRACE I pour out to those who come to adore My Eucharistic presence is immeasurable by man and feared by evil.

EVIL HATES love because love is pure, love is true and love is a divine gift full of grace and power. It is love that overcomes all evil; true love in Me.

REMEMBER NO matter how strong evil is My love is stronger.

St. Michael Archangel

IT WAS by the power of God's love that lucifer was cast from heaven and it is by this same power he will be cast from the lives of people when they embrace and accept God's love and reject evil.

Matthew 8:26 — why are you terrified, o you of little faith.

St. Thomas the Apostle

THE EVIL one does not doubt in the absolute power of God's divine love and neither should mankind.

St. Louis

POWER WITHOUT compassion is nothing but pride.
Power without love is nothing but evil.
Power without God is nothing but weakness.

Esther 4:30 — The power of the wicked.

Union

Jesus

IN TRUE union with Me a person cannot be overcome by evil.

War

God the Father

IN WAR sin grows. In war hate festers. In war evil abounds. No matter what the reason, war is evil and in war sin and hatred become the norm as goodness is forgotten. War is a terrible blight upon the earth that needs to be rejected by all and never accepted by any.

Jeremiah 8:11 — Peace, peace!

IN THE evil of war lies to justify killing are commonplace, lies which foolishly many believe.

War is not My way nor My Son, Jesus' way, nor My Holy Spirit's way; it is the way of evil.

Jesus

The spiritual war continues in every moment so always be aware that evil is there but be secure in the knowledge that in Me evil is beaten and in Me you become the victor.

Psalm 31:24 — The lord protects the loyal.

Evil laughs when war exists.
Evil smiles as lives are lost.
Evil is happy at the misery war brings into lives knowing evil will be the only victor no matter what the result.

Baruch 3:4 — and the evils cling to us.

When peace reigns in the world evil will be defeated and life will be happy. When love reigns in the world hatred will disappear and wars will end. When My love reigns peace will come to earth and people will live the happy lives they are meant to.

Psalm 115:15 — Blessed by The Lord.

Evil runs free in war.

Evil succeeds in war even when it seems good has won.

Peace is My way, war is evil's way.

To believe in war as a solution to problems is to believe that evil can solve problems instead of realizing evil only creates and increases problems.

Holy Spirit

THOSE WHO go to war go into the arms of evil. The spirit of peace needs to be embraced by mankind not the spirit of war as it is the spirit of war that comes from the spirit of evil. I AM the Holy Spirit of peace, embrace Me.

Weakness

God the Father

EVIL IS only strong when mankind is weak.

Jesus

IT IS when the mind is tired evil works hard to lead a person into sin through their weakness. Be aware of this so as to avoid sinning.

A WEAK person is one who succumbs to evil and sin.

NO ONE can ever be taken from Me by evil unless they allow it to happen.

EVIL IS weak in the face of My love and in the face of the love of those who are truly devoted to Me.

Mother Mary

IN THE love of God a person, no matter how weak they may be, can overcome all evil.

EVIL DRAWS good people to do bad by working on their fears, desires and weaknesses. God draws bad people to do good by working to overcome their fears, to answer their true desires and to strengthen their weak souls.

St. Teresa of Avila

BE FIRM in your love of God and know there is nothing evil can do to destroy your love. Only you can do that by succumbing to the evil one.

Wronged

God the Father

REMEMBER WHEN people wrong you forgive them and do not seek revenge otherwise you too then do wrong and evil wins.

WHEN OTHERS do you wrong respond by only doing what is right so that evil does not draw you into its web of sin.

DELIVERED BY THE CROSS

My first spiritual director, Father Dickinson suggested I share this experience even though normally I do not share my personal experiences of this type.
The Lord said to me during Mass, "Come to the cross through the Eucharist." Then in confession as penance Father Dickinson said to pray a decade of the Rosary meditating on the crucifixion. I felt The Lord's pain, but I also saw in every Mass was the sacrifice of Jesus and that when Jesus united with me in communion that not only was He bringing me deep into His heart and filling me with His love but that also He was allowing me to unite with Him on the cross. I saw that in the bread and wine was Jesus bleeding on the cross and that if I opened my heart in a desire to love Him more, He would show me His love in another way from the cross and that in each Eucharist as Jesus' sacrifice is revealed that I could, by His grace, live it with Him. I saw that to eat of this bread and drink of this wine was also an acceptance to carry the cross in my life in whichever way Jesus offered it to me. That in each Eucharist if I offered Jesus the cross I carried it would be bring me closer to His suffering and to a deeper experience of His love.

Accepting Crosses

God the Father

EVERY CROSS no matter how small can open a person to great graces when they accept their crosses in love of My Son Jesus and offer it to Me in love by the grace of My Holy Spirit.

MANY CROSSES are given to the few who are willing to carry them but then so are many graces.

Jesus

ACCEPT YOUR crosses in love just as I accepted Mine in love.

ACCEPT YOUR crosses lovingly and gratefully and grow in grace.

EVERY CROSS in life can be a grace or burden. People have the choice; accept it in My love and it is a grace; reject it in pride and it becomes a burden.

Holy Spirit

DO NOT reject any gift others offer you in love. Accept them in love even when it is a sacrifice to do so, offering those sacrifices to Jesus on the cross in love and accepting in love of Him any cross you may have to carry even when it comes because of the generosity of others.

Barriers

St. Benedict

EVIL MAY try to block the way to heaven but with the cross of Christ as your weapon you can destroy any barrier evil places before you.

Blessing

God the Father

BE GRATEFUL for every cross for in each one is a true blessing.

REMEMBER, EVERY cross you carry is a blessing that opens you to more grace when you carry it willingly and in love.

EVERY CROSS is a blessing not a curse because in each cross is a key to more grace when a person accepts their cross in love and in love offers it to Me for the good of others.

Jesus

TO BE given a cross by Me is a great blessing indeed.

IF YOU make My way of the cross your way of life you will be truly blessed.

LET EVERY cross become a blessing by offering them to Me in love.

SEE YOUR work for Me a blessing, not a cross, no matter how hard it is.

WITH EVERY cross is a blessing, remember that.

Mother Mary

WITH EVERY cross comes blessings and if people truly look they will see them.

PRAISE GOD from your heart in love for even the smallest blessings and the largest crosses.

St. John of the Cross

IN CHRIST, Our Lord, no cross is a curse, it is always a blessing.

Blindness

Jesus

EVEN MY divine act of love on the cross is not enough to melt some hearts for they do not see it in their blindness.

FROM THE cross I saw every soul that has been created and I knew them; sadly many did not know Me.

2 Maccabees 4:35 — Not only the Jews but many people of other nations as well.

Carrying the Cross

God the Father

EVERY CROSS you carry do so joyfully knowing it is for the love of Me and the love of others you carry it and that you do not carry it alone as My Son Jesus carries it with you.

ALWAYS HELP others where possible to carry their crosses.

MANY OF the crosses you carry are given to you in love by Me and accept them in love of Me.

IT IS the way you carry your crosses that shows if you truly try to imitate My Son Jesus or not. If you carry them lovingly, forgivingly and quietly in love of Me and in love of others, then you carry them as He carried His cross. If you carry your crosses with grumbling, complaining or seeking attention for what you do, then you only think of self and are nothing like My Son Jesus in His suffering.

Jesus

CARRYING A cross is part of being a follower of Mine. To suffer for your faith is a way of imitating Me. To be persecuted for your love of Me shows you are truly Mine.

Romans 9:33 — whoever believes
2 Chronicles 18:15 — in the name of the lord.

WITH EVERY cross a follower of Mine carries comes the strength from Me to carry them.

As you carry your crosses remember I am carrying you and your crosses.

Bear your crosses bravely in imitation of Me.

Carry the crosses in love of Me and in love of others.

On the cross I carried your pride and in My merciful love I offer you from the cross the strength to overcome it.

In love of others carry your crosses just as I carried Mine.

As you carry your crosses think of how I carried Mine and think of how your crosses are a small part of the cross I carried.

My cross resides in every heart that loves Me for every heart that truly loves Me longs to cling to My cross and in some way carry it with Me.

There are few to do My work and much to do. Therefore the few have to carry the many crosses that should be shared by all. It is by carrying these crosses that many will be saved and this will bring its rewards to the few when they come to heaven.

Mark 15:21 — Carry his cross.

Every cross you bear for Me will bring great grace for you and through you for others.

There will be many crosses in life so let Me carry them with you by offering them to Me in grateful and joyful love.

It is through the crosses you carry for Me that many graces are granted.

THERE ARE many crosses to be carried but not many who want to carry them; be one that does.

WITH EVERY cross I give a person to carry I give the person the strength to carry it.

I CARRIED not only your sins to the cross but also your love.

Mother Mary

MY SON Jesus showed His love for you on the cross, now show your love for Him in the crosses you carry.

REMEMBER THE crosses God calls you to carry are full of blessings.

THE LITTLE crosses you carry in love bring great graces because of that love.

THE FEW who truly love God carry their crosses in love for the many who do not.

St. Paul

DO NOT think of the crosses you carry, rather think of the graces you receive.

Philippians 4:23 — The grace of The Lord Jesus Christ.

St. Teresa of Avila

THE CROSSES Christ, Our Lord, asks you to carry may be heavy but the grace He gives you to do so in Him is strong enough to carry any and all crosses.

St. John of the Cross

> WHEN GOD offers a person a cross to carry if they accept it willingly and in love, then God pours out grace beyond the weight of the cross, grace for all the world just as His cross was for all the world.
>
> IF YOU believe that in almost every moment of your life you are carrying your own cross then life will become a misery instead of the wonderful gift of love it was meant to be. If, however, you believe Jesus is carrying your cross with you, then the joy of His sacrificial love will touch your very soul. Then even through the most difficult times you will be happy in His love and show His love in all you do discovering what a gift God has given to you.
>
> *Psalm 107:22 — Let them offer a sacrifice in thanks, declare his works with shouts of joy.*
>
> SEE EVERY cross God gives you as crosses of love and carry them in love thanking God for such blessings.
>
> TO CARRY a cross in your life for Christ is one of the greatest gifts you can be given.
>
> ON THE cross Jesus showed His love for you. As you carry your crosses show your love for Him.
>
> *Titus 2:14 — who gave himself for us*

St. Stephen

> NO SACRIFICE is too great for a person who truly loves God and no cross carried for Him and for others is a misery, it is a joy.

Comfort

Jesus

KNOWING YOUR love comforted Me on the cross.

Psalm 119:50 this is my comfort.

OFFERING YOUR discomfort to Me brings Me comfort in My suffering on the cross as it shows your true love of Me.

Courage

God the Father

IT TAKES courage to keep living as I ask. The courage My Son Jesus, gives to His followers in His love that was shown on the cross.

Difficulties

Jesus

IF THE crosses were not difficult they would not be crosses.

WITH EACH struggle, with each cross, with each difficulty a person can grow in grace by persevering in love of Me.

Romans 12:1 — a living sacrifice, holy and pleasing to God.

BE A little more understanding of others and appreciate the struggles they face and their efforts to overcome them, do not only think of your crosses.

EVERY CROSS brings many graces, remember that as you struggle with your crosses.

IT IS through your sacrifices much good is achieved. Remember this when you struggle with your crosses.

IT WAS painful on the cross to look upon humanity and see how difficult it was for mankind to accept My sacrifice and My forgiveness. But it was joyful to see that one day many would accept and that many would know My love.

WHEN THERE are difficulties do not complain, instead thank Me for them and offer them to Me on the cross and then you will find they become graces not problems.

WHEN THE day is long and arduous think of how My day on the cross was.

St. Theresa of Avila

As I travelled I encountered many obstacles and many difficulties but each time I thought of Jesus carrying His cross on the road to Calvary and I found the strength to carry on. Do the same and find the strength you need.

Darkness

Jesus

I AM the light of the world that illuminates the souls lost in darkness, bringing them to eternal light through My suffering and death on the cross and My resurrection from the grave.

Embrace the Cross

God the Father

TO SERVE Me brings crosses; embrace them in love of Me, do not push them away in fear.

CLING TO the cross and cling to life.

EVERY CROSS you are given, if you embrace them with love, become ways of being open to more grace and of growing in grace.

THE SUFFERING My Son, Jesus, bore on the cross was the suffering of the sins of mankind.

THE LOVE My Son, Jesus, showed on the cross was the love of God for sinful mankind.

THE FORGIVENESS My Son, Jesus, offered on the cross was the forgiveness all of mankind needs to embrace if it is to come to the eternal love of God in heaven.

ON THE cross My Son, Jesus, reached out to mankind in an embrace of love that spans eternity.

Jesus

With My love as your strength embrace any cross you are asked to carry and climb any mountain placed before you.

On the cross I opened My arms to embrace all people in My love. In the lives of those who love Me they must also open their arms to embrace all people in My love united with their love.

Deuteronomy 22:3 — You shall do the same.

When a person tries to live as I ask they must expect crosses and welcome the crosses not reject them.

Cling to My cross and cling to your salvation.

Embrace every cross in love and do not push them away in self-pity.

With each cross comes a grace and if you embrace that cross in love of Me then even more graces are given.

Truly to help others you must deny yourself just as I did and you must be prepared to embrace your cross just as I did.

Every cross is a blessing so do not fear them nor push them away. Embrace your crosses as I embraced My cross and I will give you the grace to carry them with the strength of My love.

Embrace every cross in love of Me and of others and grow in My grace.

Mother Mary

> THE CROSS should be embraced in trusting love not in doubts and fear.
>
> EACH CROSS, a grace. Each cross, a gift. Each cross, a sign of love. When you can see each cross in these ways then you start to see the truth and in doing so embrace each cross joyfully for me.

St. John of the Cross

> HOLDING ON to the cross of Jesus, Our Lord, does not bring misery, it brings true happiness to life.
>
> *2 Corinthians 13:4 — for indeed he was crucified out of weakness, but lives by the power of God.*
>
> DO NOT reject the crosses God gives you; embrace them in the love of God.

Forgiveness

Jesus

> ALL PEOPLE are offered forgiveness from the mercy of My Father by the grace of the Holy Spirit and in My sacrificial love shown on the cross.
>
> ALL FORGIVING grace throughout time came from My sacrifice on the cross.
>
> *Luke 24:47 — The forgiveness of sins.*

EVEN WHEN others mock Me show them love and forgiveness just as I did on the cross.

MY MERCY is offered to all. My forgiveness is there for all. My love is shown to all and it is seen on the cross.

Mother Mary

TO SHED blood for love is what my Son, Jesus did in love on the cross. The precious blood of forgiveness that all should bathe in if they want to find eternal peace.

St. Helena

I FOUND the cross of Christ before I went to Jerusalem. I found it in my heart when Jesus exposed His love to me and offered me His forgiveness.

From the Cross

Jesus

FROM THE cross I looked out upon the world and offered it peace in Me. That offer is still there just waiting for mankind to accept it. When the world does it will be at peace and My love will fill all hearts with joy.

Luke 17:30 — the day the son of man is revealed.

AS I looked down upon the world from the cross I saw all the pain and all the hurt mankind brought upon itself through sin. Then I opened My heart to lift this burden from My family on earth. All it takes is mankind coming to My open heart to be cleansed in the blood and water that flowed from My wounded heart. This cleansing is there for all and is found within the sacraments where in My mercy I reach out in forgiveness and in love. Where I offer each person the opportunity to be forgiven and to be filled with My Body and My Blood and the divine water of My cleansing love.

Ezekiel 2:8 — what I shall give you...

WITH MY gifts and graces comes My cross.

Faith

Jesus

TO UNDERSTAND fully My sacrifice on the cross is not possible in a lifetime but to believe in it completely is, and that is called faith.

Giving

Jesus

ON THE cross I completely gave Myself for you. In the Eucharist I completely give Myself to you. In return I only ask you give your life completely to Me.

Guilt

God the Father

MANY PEOPLE were involved in the crucifixion of My son, Jesus, not just those you read of in Holy Scripture. Everyone who has sinned contributed to the suffering of My Son, Jesus. So to lay the blame on the few who are written about is unjust and unwise for it hides the part each one has played when they have sinned. When someone else is held to account for the suffering of My Son, Jesus, then it is much easier for those who feel no guilt to be led into the sin of pride and through that into more and more sin. All sinners share in the guilt just as all sinners can share in the forgiveness by recognizing their part in the suffering of their Saviour and then coming to the cross repenting of their sins.

Revelations 1:5 — to him who loves us and has freed us from our sins by his blood.

Heart of the Cross

Jesus

THE BLOOD of heaven that flowed from My side stemmed the evil tide. The sacred water of love that poured out from My side, said to all mankind, in My heart you can hide.
The grace of God running down from where I hung on the cross, said to all, your soul need not be lost.

Zechariah 1:16 — I will turn to Jerusalem in mercy.

As My heart opened on the cross My mercy swept through eternity reaching out to all those in need and offering them salvation. My mercy is there in every moment for every person and I call from My heart for each one to come to Me and accept it.

Micah 7:18 — *The God who removes guilt and pardons sin.*

Open your heart to all in love just as I do and I did on the cross.

On the cross I bared My heart in love, through your suffering do the same.

St. Paul

God opened His heart on the cross, calling out, offering His love. All He asks in return is that people open their hearts to receive that love within and find eternal bliss in His call.

St. Margaret Mary

The heart of the Saviour poured out His sacredness over the whole earth when it was pierced on the cross.

Heavy Crosses

God the Father

WHEN THE crosses seem heavy, remember how heavy My Son Jesus' cross was.

NO CROSS is too heavy for those who truly love Me and live for My love.

REMEMBER EVERY cross you carry is not as heavy as the cross My Son, Jesus, carried for mankind.

Jesus

NO CROSS will be too heavy for those who truly love Me.

NO CROSS should be too heavy for a follower of Mine if they truly trust in Me and rely on My strength to carry their crosses.

WHEN THE crosses are heavy remember to ask the Holy Spirit to help you with them.

WHEN A person loves Me with a true love then no cross is too heavy to carry in love of Me.

IT IS when the crosses are heavy you can show how strong your love of Me is by thanking Me for them from your heart.

WHEN THE crosses are heavy remember Mine was heavier.

IF YOU do your best for Me and if in doing so it causes you to carry heavy crosses, know the best is waiting for you with Me in eternity and accept your crosses joyfully in the knowledge of what is to come.

WHEN A loved one leaves in death it hurts because you love them. So see the pain as part of love, as a sign of love and as the truth of love, not as a burden or a cross that is too heavy.

WHEN THE crosses are heavy remember how heavy Mine was. When the crosses are heavy remember Mine was heavier.

IT IS when the crosses are heavy you can show how strong your love of Me is by thanking Me for them from your heart.

IF YOU allow the small crosses to become big ones you will weigh yourself down with heavy crosses and unnecessary burdens.

WHEN YOU accept the heaviest cross in love of Me you imitate Me as I accepted the heaviest cross for love of you.

THE TRAGEDIES of life are part of living but how a person faces them affects how the person continues to live. If they are faced in God life is not full of sorrow, bitterness or the seeking of revenge. If the tragedies are faced in self then life can become a heavy cross too hard to bear for the person and those they are in contact with.

Mother Mary

THE CROSSES you carry may seem heavy but compared to My Son Jesus' cross they are light indeed.

St. John of the Cross

NO CROSS is too heavy for those who truly love Jesus, The Lord, and who truly are prepared to sacrifice for Him in love.

NO CROSS is too heavy if you carry it in the love of Christ, Our Lord.

St. Andrew

IN THE cross of Jesus is one of the greatest blessings of God's love. Sadly, so many do not believe this and in doing so do not realize this will bring them a heavy eternal cross.

St. Francis Xavier

TO SERVE God is a grace given to a person in love. To serve God is a sign of how much God cares for and trusts the person with His work.
To serve God may at times seem like a heavy burden but in these moments remember God gives the person this grace so that they can be rewarded with His eternal love then surely no cross is too heavy and no burden too difficult to carry.

1 Corinthians 9:17 — Do so willingly.
Isaiah 58:9 — Then you shall call and The Lord will answer, you will cry for help, and he will say: Here I am!

Holy Week / Good Friday

Jesus

IN THIS Holy Week focus on My cross and the love I showed for mankind and then see how in your crosses you can do the same.

Mother Mary   Good Friday

THE AGONY of the cross was rewarded by the salvation of souls.

Genesis 49:24 — by the power of the mighty one.

MY HEART broke as I watched my Son, Jesus, suffer and die on the cross before me. My heart broke as I saw mankind kill its Saviour. My heart broke as I heard the people abuse and reject their God.
Then as I looked at Jesus before me I knew this was meant to be and that it would be through my broken heart that many would come to find the Sacred Heart of my Son, Jesus, and find salvation there for them. I then began to cry tears of joy as well as tears of sorrow as I thanked God for His mercy and I thanked God for His wonderful gift He gave to me.

Sirach 7:15 — which was ordained by the most high.

Humility

Jesus

HUMBLE YOURSELF before others if you want to imitate Me as this is what I did on the cross.

ACCEPT HUMBLY your crosses as pride will only make them heavier.

MANKIND'S PRIDE nailed Me to the cross and My humility overcame the cross and revealed the grace to show that humble love is more powerful than prideful hatred.

Mother Mary

REMEMBER IN the crosses a person carries there are great graces if the person seeks them in humble and accepting love of God's will.

In the Garden

Jesus

IN THE Garden of Gethsemane I endured all of mankind's suffering as I embraced it in merciful love carrying it to the cross with Me so that through My cross mankind could be comforted, healed and forgiven.

IN THE Garden of Gethsemane I opened My heart and took all of mankind's sins deep inside. I then wrapped My loving heart around all the pain, the turmoil, the confusion, the hurt and the hatred and in love sweated droplets of My precious blood before

I carried all of this evil with Me as I endured the torment and the agony of the cross in My victory over all evil.

MY HEART remains open to all mankind and if people will place their hearts in Mine then My loving heart will wrap around their hearts and protect them from all evil as they unite in My loving victory over evil.

IN THE garden I knew each person's sins and I carried all the pain of them. Then on the cross in My pain I overcame all sin. In My death I reached out to each person offering them salvation in Me and with My resurrection I call all people to new life in Me eternally.

St. Peter Apostle

IN THE garden of Gethsemane The Lord Jesus opened His heart and soul taking all of mankind's suffering into His being. That is why in their suffering all people can turn to The Lord, Jesus, and unite with Him in the garden allowing His peace and strength to enter into them. Then seeing that just as The Lord, Jesus, carried the cross to Calvary He is carrying them and will not let them carry their crosses alone. Knowing too that when they face death people can turn to The Lord Who is waiting on the cross to embrace them in His love to resurrect them in Him and to lift them to heaven in His love.

St. Theresa (The little Flower)

IN THE garden of Gethsemane The Lord took all of mankind's sins on His heart. He took all the pain and suffering from even the most horrible of sins onto Himself. Because of this He sweated tears of love for mankind as His holy blood poured out through His skin.

In each stroke of the whip the physical sins of mankind cut through the divine flesh exposing the deep love of God.

As the thorns pierced the head of The Holy One all the sinful thoughts of mankind brought forth a trickle of mercy for everyone to share in.

Within the weight of the cross was all the spiritual sins of mankind whose rejection of God would not and could not stop The Lord carrying them in love of man.

Yes, the sins were so heavy that He fell but in the divine strength of God, The Lord rose up and continued to carry even the most grievous sins for those He loved.

On the cross as The Lord was lifted on high, He raised up the sins of mankind with Him and in Him, imploring The Father to accept His sacrifice and to forgive mankind for their wrongs.

With an open heart He washed the world in His suffering and offered all forgiveness in and through Him.

Then in the glory of the resurrection The Lord showed the truth of His divinity and the truth of His invitation for all to join Him in eternal love in heaven.

The truth that all should believe and respond to.

Looking at the Cross

Jesus

THE LOVE I showed on the cross I showed to all but sadly not all look and see it.

LOOK TO the cross and see how I gave all that I AM willingly and lovingly.

LOOK UPON each cross you are given with love, as that is how I looked upon My cross.

St. John Apostle

THE LOVE of God is mysterious and wonderful. It is a mystery mankind can never understand on earth but can look and wonder at each time it looks to the cross.

St. Mary Magdala

WATCHING THE Lord, Jesus suffer and die was the most difficult thing I had to do in my life but as I looked into His eyes on the cross He poured out the strength for me to endure the terrible misery I felt within. He will do the same to all those who in their misery look to Him on the cross in love, seeking the strength and help that only He can give.

St. John of the Cross

EACH PERSON'S cross at times to them can seem so large, but when you look to the cross of Jesus it becomes clear your own cross is not so large at all.

Love of the Cross

Jesus

IT IS true love that lifts mankind above evil as evil cannot know true love, cannot exist in true love and cannot overcome true love. I am true love and on the cross I showed My love, now in your life show Me yours.

St. John the Apostle

THE SAVIOUR of the world hung on the cross calling out His love for all people. The Saviour of the world hung in agony on the cross carrying the suffering caused by the sin of all people.
The Saviour of the world hung until death on the cross to show all people He loved them and that in His love He was prepared to carry all of their suffering and prepared to forgive them their sins. All He asks in return is that people love Him.

St. John of the Cross

THE LOVE that The Lord Jesus showed on the cross is both divine and human. While people cannot have that divine love for others, they can have that human love and can show it to others in imitation of our suffering Lord by asking the Divine Spirit to give them the grace to do so.

John 11:36 — see how he loved.

Mercy

Jesus

MY SACRIFICE on the cross is an eternal moment that spans eternity and fills it with My mercy.

MY LOVE was shown on the cross and continues to be shown in My mercy.

Holy Spirit

THE TRUE spirit of man can only be found through the mercy shown on the cross.

Mother Mary

MY SON Jesus' sacrifice on the cross was and is an eternal moment that pours out His mercy into every moment of eternity.

St. Benedict

TO CARRY a cross is a gift God gives so you can share in His mercy.

More Crosses

Jesus

SIN BRINGS many more crosses than living to My way does.

Offering

Jesus

OFFERING YOUR sorrow to Me on the cross can bring you the strength you need in sad times.

LET THE pain in your heart go by giving it to Me on the cross in an offering of love.

St. Mary Magdela

EVERY PERSON on earth no matter how good they appear is a sinner and every person on earth is offered the opportunity of being a saint in heaven by accepting the grace of God into their lives that Jesus, The Lord, poured out from the cross.

Luke 1:50 — his mercy
Sirach 40:24 — that rescues
Acts 22:16 — your sins washed away

Proclaim

St. John the Baptist

TO PROCLAIM the greatness of God is the call to all followers of Jesus, none are excepted. To proclaim the love of God for all people is the duty of the followers of Jesus, none are excluded. To proclaim the forgiveness that Jesus offers to all from the cross is the obligation of all followers of Jesus, none should deny it.

Isaiah 66:14 — his servants
Ephesians 5:30 — because we are members of his body

Rewarded

Jesus

I WILL not let people's efforts go unrewarded and I will not forget the crosses people carry in love of Me.

Mother Mary

EVERY CROSS, every struggle, every battle, you carry for God will be rewarded with great grace.

Salvation

God the Father

THE CROSS of My Son, Jesus is to be loved, venerated and exalted, for it is through His cross all can find salvation.

Jesus

JUST AS at the time of Moses when many were drawn into sin because of their struggles in the desert, today many struggle in a spiritual desert and are drawn into sin. Just as Moses brought The Word of God down from the mountain to save the sinners My followers should bring Me and My forgiving cross down from the hill of Calvary and into the hearts of sinners so the sinner can be saved in Me, the living Word of God.

HANGING ON the cross I looked into eternity and saw all who would be saved by My sacrifice and it brought Me great joy and comfort. I saw too all who rejected salvation in Me and this brought Me great sadness and weighed heavily on My heart. With a heavy heart I cried out 'Father, forgive them for they know not what they do.' This cry echoes in eternity touching the eternal heart of My Father Who wants to pour out His mercy upon those who will ask for it.

Shadow of the Cross

God the Father

IN THE shadow of the cross know you are secure.

Jesus

UNDER THE shadow of My cross is a secure haven for all.

THE SHADOW of the cross falls upon the world covering it with My sacrificial love. Offering to all who will stand in the shadow of love peace and security now and forever.

St. Andrew

THE SHADOW of the cross covers the world and those who stand in it in love will find eternal peace. Those who do not, those who reject it, will find eternal suffering.

THE CROSS of Jesus casts its shadow over all people. The cross of Jesus pours out forgiveness on all people. The cross of Jesus is a sign of love for all people. Jesus' loving forgiveness is for all people, as He has said many times: It is only evil that casts doubt over this.

1 Timothy 2:6 — *Who gave himself as a ransom for all.*

Suffering of and with The Lord

God the Father

As My Son, Jesus, suffered on the cross He carried all of your suffering with Him.

Think of the gentle love of My Son, Jesus, nailed to the cross and expect as you show His gentle love to others that you will suffer too.

Jesus

The cross joins heaven and earth. The cross unites divine suffering and human suffering. The cross unites My divine suffering with that of the earth and joins each person's pain to Mine making their crosses heavenly gifts.

Wisdom 14:7 — For blessed is the wood through which justice comes about.

My sacrifice on the cross was finite yet it was infinite. It was finite because it happened on a certain day at a certain time. It is infinite because it spans all the suffering, all the pain and all the sin from the beginning of time until the end of time, offering forgiveness to all people. So My suffering fills not only the time it happened but fills all of time and all of eternity. A divine mystery.

On the cross I wore the crown of suffering while in heaven I wear the crown of eternal kingship and glory.
All those who wear the crown of suffering for following Me and calling Me their king will be crowned by Me in heaven with eternal glory.

WHEN YOU hurt from doing My work you join Me on the cross.

NO ONE who loves Me should fear suffering but should embrace it willingly in Me, so that they can be united in My suffering on the cross.

AS I suffered on the cross I poured out My love eternally. As I suffered on the cross I showered creation with mercy. As I suffered on the cross I called out to mankind here I AM for you. On the cross of love the mercy of God was offered to all of mankind throughout time, showing that God loves His creation and will not deny them His mercy.

Jeremiah 15:19 — if you repent.

THE POOR and the wealthy; both in need.
The poor in need of food, of money, of medicine, of housing, of security, of help and of understanding. The wealthy in need of sight to see the suffering of the poor, in need of hearts to help the poor. In need of souls prepared to sacrifice for the poor. In need of lives given to serve the poor. In need of understanding.
The poor need to understand that in their suffering they can join with Me on the cross and share in the graces I shower upon the world from the cross. The graces that can bring them to eternal peace and happiness with Me in heaven.
The wealthy need to understand that unless they share what they have with the poor and stop the greed and selfishness that is in many of their lives, eternal poverty will be theirs as they suffer in the darkness of hell. It will then be they who are begging for help and that the answer will be the same for them as the answer they gave to the poor on earth.

Matthew 3:15 — For thus it is fitting.

SHOWERING YOUR love upon others is what you are meant to do even when you suffer. When I suffered on the cross I showered all with My love and you too, as a follower of Mine, are meant to follow in this way.

ON THE cross I glorified God and by offering their pain in love to God those who suffer can do the same.

Acts 13:48 — *Glorified the word of The Lord.*

IN MY pain on the cross I knew your pain and I embraced it in love pouring out the grace for you to carry your pain joyfully in Me if you so desire.

THE ACT of love I did on the cross is an example to all people not to fear suffering and death but to know that in Me suffering can become blessed and that death is defeated.

THE SORROW of love you feel is the sharing of the pain of love I endured for you and for all on the cross.

Mother Mary

WHEN YOU feel pain, if you offer it to my Son, Jesus on the cross, as you share it with Him, you share in His grace to carry your hurt.

St. John of the Cross

TO SUFFER for Christ is the greatest cross a person can receive for it is being one with Christ, Our Lord, on the cross.

St. Lucy

THERE IS no pain a human can endure that compares to the pain Our Lord, Jesus, carried to and on the cross.

The Eucharist

God the Father

SATAN IS terrified of the Holy Eucharist, that is why he tries to stop it. He is terrified that people will be filled with My Son Jesus' divine love and the power of His divine victory on the cross and in the resurrection. This is why the evil one works hard to sow doubt and disbelief in the Holy Eucharist. Evil does not want the world filled with people living in My Son, Jesus, in the Eucharist. The evil one knows this would bring salvation in My Son, Jesus, to many more and would save many souls.

Jesus

MY LOVE was shown on the cross and is shown in every Eucharist.

The Sign

Jesus

MY CROSS, My sign of My love for you and for all. In love of Me make your crosses signs of your love for Me and for others.

Mother Mary

THE CROSS is the sign of God's forgiving love not God's condemnation.

St. John of the Cross

THE CROSS the true sign of love.

THE SIGN of how you love Jesus, The Lord, can be seen in how you carry your crosses for Him.

Touched

St. Helena

ONCE A person is touched by the cross of Christ their lives are changed forevermore.

Victory

God the Father

ETERNAL GOODNESS was victorious over evil as My Son, Jesus, The Good One, confronted and defeated evil on the cross.

Jesus

EVIL STALKS the world and believes it can win the war for the souls of mankind. The war has already been won by My sacrifice on the cross and whether evil accepts this or not does not matter for evil has been defeated and it is only those who give themselves willingly to the loser who will be lost.

2 Chronicles 35:21 — *he will destroy you.*

THERE IS a constant battle in every life between good and evil and in every battle good will triumph if the person clings to Me, to My goodness and to My victory on the cross.

EVIL WAS defeated on the cross and people need to look no further than the cross to achieve victory over evil in their lives.

Isaiah 66:14 — *the lord's power shall be known to his servants.*

MY AGONY; the agony of love.
My cross; the cross of love.
My death; the death of love.
The agony I suffered on the cross until death showed that death could not defeat love and when I rose on the third day love was shown to have defeated death.

THE JOY, the pain, the passion. The joy of saving souls was there through the pain as I showed from the cross how passionately I love mankind.

Titus 2:14 — *Who gave himself for us to deliver us.*

St. John of the Cross

ON THE cross evil was defeated by love, in life it is the same.

1 Maccabees 4:33 — *Those who love.*
Jeremiah 50:45 — *The Lord.*
Psalm 118:7 — *Shall look in triumph.*

St. Michael the Archangel

YOU CANNOT be defeated by evil if you cling in true love to the victory of Jesus on the cross and in the resurrection.

Wounded for Love

Jesus

MY WOUNDS were opened to all on the cross so that all, through My loving wounds, could find their way home to heaven.

THE GREAT love I showed on the cross I showed to and for all.

LETTERS

Let Your Faith Define You Aug 13, 2008

SO OFTEN Catholics change their beliefs to suit themselves and the world because their catholic faith opposes what they want or what they think should happen in life. These changes may be little or large but they all have the same result and that is to make what the person believes no longer Catholic and just another worldly way.

To be truly Catholic is to live to what the Church teaches and not to put one's own personal preferences before that. Some have forgotten that when the Church speaks on faith, morals and life that it is God's Holy Spirit speaking. Some have forgotten or reject the authority that Christ, Our Lord, gave to St. Peter and through him to all the popes. Instead, they put their own authority and judgement before that of the Church. This is fraught with danger for surely human desires will influence people's judgement and may lead people into the acceptance of what is wrong. This too is a reflection of mankind's pride where people often believe they know better than God. The same pride that Lucifer has!

To live as a Catholic means to live humbly in obedience to the will of God as it is shown by God through His Holy Catholic and Apostolic Church. Anything less diminishes a person's faith and opens the person to serious error and misunderstandings of God's will. True faith is defined by a complete acceptance of God's will as explained by The Commandments and the teachings of the Church even when a person does not understand the reasons for them. To follow and accept only what a person understands leaves a great void in faith as the pride that says, 'I will only accept what I know to be true', closes the heart to God. What arrogance it is to accept only what can be proven or what fits in with what a person perceives to be true, for surely our human minds do not know everything and do not understand everything. There is so much in existence that we know so little about and have still to unravel. Yet mankind so easily denies God and His eternal truth. Many Catholics are guilty of this by putting self before God and changing their faith so that it fits in comfortably with their life.

Our faith is meant to define us in the way that our lives are lived with the faith as given by God and explained by His Holy Catholic and Apostolic Church. Every decision we make, every action we do and every word we speak are meant to be expressions of God's will so that those who look upon us see the truth of God's love and are drawn to His love through us and away from the bitterness of evil.

Let us reflect on the early Church and it's obedience to God's will even until death and how by the grace of God the sacrifices made then defined the Church in the world and showed the beauty of God's love to all.

Appropriateness of receiving the Eucharist by Catholics who support abortion   Oct 9, 2008

IT HAS been asked several times about Catholics who support abortion and the receiving by them of The Lord in the Eucharist and if this is permissible or appropriate. Of course the first point of reference to this for all Catholics should be Church teachings and statements on this.

THE CATECHISM of the Catholic Church states:

1385: to respond to this invitation we must prepare ourselves for so great and so holy a moment. St. Paul urges us to examine our conscience: "Whoever, therefore, eats the bread or drinks the cup of The Lord in an unworthy manner will be guilty of profaning the body and the blood of The Lord. Let a man examine himself and so eat of the bread and drink of the cup. For anyone who eats and drinks without discerning the body eats and drinks judgement upon himself." Anyone conscious of a grave sin must receive the sacrament of Reconciliation before coming to communion.

1415: Anyone who desires to receive Christ in Eucharistic communion must be in a state of grace. Anyone aware of having sinned mortally must not receive communion without having received absolution in the sacrament of penance.

POPE BENEDICT XVI wrote a letter in June 2004 to the US bishops when he was still Cardinal Ratzinger stating the principles of being worthy to receive The Lord in Communion. Cardinal Ratzinger, the head of the Congregation for the Doctrine of the Faith at that time, said that strong and open supporters of abortion should be denied Eucharistic communion for being guilty of a grave sin.

SOME OF the Bishops' comments:

(Zenit) – New York prelates are urging citizens to get informed about the platforms of Congressional and state candidates, since they say many moral issues are decided at the state level. This was one of the points highlighted in a statement released last week called "Our Cherished Right, Our Solemn Duty."

THE PRELATES first recalled that life issues are the most important criteria when it comes to casting a ballot.

"It is the rare candidate who will agree with the Church on every issue," they acknowledged. "But [...] not every issue is of equal moral gravity. The inalienable right to life of every innocent human person outweighs other concerns where Catholics may use prudential judgment, such as how best to meet the needs of the poor or to increase access to health care for all."

"The right to life is the right through which all others flow. To the extent candidates reject this fundamental right by supporting an objective evil, such as legal abortion, euthanasia or embryonic stem cell research, Catholics should consider them less acceptable for public office."

UNITED STATES Conference of Catholic Bishops

It would be refreshing if we could find candidates whose records, party platforms, and personal commitments embody the full range of the Church's social teaching, reasonable as that teaching is. Unfortunately that seldom happens. That is why we must have a well-formed conscience capable of giving each issue its proper moral weight and making other important distinctions and judgments. For example, a Catholic may never vote for candidates precisely because they advocate and advance intrinsic moral evils like abortion; to do so is to cooperate formally (intentionally) with a grave evil. And while "Faithful Citizenship" acknowledges that one may vote for a politician who supports pro-abortion policies "only for truly grave moral reasons," a conscientious voter must question what grave moral issue rises to the level of nearly 49 million lives lost to the evil of abortion.

> *In Scranton, Pa., every Catholic attending Mass this weekend will hear a special homily about the election next month: Bishop Joseph Martino has ordered every priest in the diocese to read a letter warning that voting for a supporter of abortion rights amounts to endorsing "homicide." "Being 'right' on taxes, education, health care, immigration and the economy fails to make up for the error of disregarding the value of a human life," the bishop wrote. "It is a tragic irony that 'pro-choice' candidates have come to support homicide – the gravest injustice a society can tolerate – in the name of 'social justice.'" [Oct 5, 2008]*

SO, FROM Holy Scripture and from church statements it is apparent that those who promote, support or vote for a politician who is pro-abortion are in a state of grave sin and should not receive The Lord in the Eucharist. Some Catholics however disagree with this and do not accept what the church says or what is said in the Holy Word of God. Some say it is their right to receive communion, however receiving The Lord is not a right but a privilege that God offers people in His love. This privilege should not be abused for as St. Paul states there are serious consequences for doing so. Those who are in a state of grave sin must have a good confession before receiving The Lord and must, after that confession, not return to their old ways. To go to confession with the intention of once having confessed to continue the bad behaviour or beliefs does not make the confession valid. Some cannot accept this and in their pride believe they know better than the Church and the Word of God not seeing that this arrogance is a serious sin in itself as the person is placing their will before that of the will of God and the will of His holy Church. The person is saying that their knowledge is greater than that of the Church and the person is rejecting the commandment of God 'Thou shalt not kill' and saying that they or those they support or follow can decide if life is valuable or not and that God has no say in this. Today many Catholics demand their rights which in truth are their wrongs but they are so blind they cannot see this as they believe more in the word of the world instead of The Word of God.

TO COME to communion in a state of grave sin makes true union with God impossible as the person holds on to a barrier between them and God which blocks unity with Christ, Our Lord. To be one with Him means to be one in the truth of His love, to be obedient to His will and to reject all sin. While the world and people's pride may make many arguments against this none of them change this eternal truth. People should think about how it hurts Our Lord, that those who profess to love Him, come with that on their hearts which is of the dark and not of the light of His love. No Catholic in a state of grave sin should ever consider partaking of The Body, Blood, Soul and Divinity of The Lord, Jesus, in the Eucharist for doing so in itself is an insult to God and to all those who live or have lived as God asks. It is time for those who support abortion in any way to realize the wrong they embrace excludes them from receiving The Divine Lord, Jesus, in the Eucharist and in humility confess their wrong and reject it from then on and in true love come and be one with and in Him in communion in the state of grace they are supposed to be in.

Christmas Message   Dec 9, 2008

THIS CHRISTMAS as we think about the coming of the Son of God to Earth and reflect on the Holy family in Bethlehem we should see in the little child Jesus, each little child created by God. Just as we love the baby Jesus, we too should love each child God blesses mankind with. Our hearts should be reaching out in love to the babies treasuring the blessing of their lives. If each one of us considers the magnificence of God's love in every baby then it will follow that our hearts will ache with love for them and we will desire only the best for each child. It too will become apparent to those, whom it is not already, how precious to God the little ones are and they will become precious to them. No longer will the destruction of babies for any reason be acceptable and no longer can a heart that loves God's little treasures support in any way the most terrible sin of abortion. No longer will thoughts of self and what a person desires for themselves and others, even if they are good intentions, be placed above the value of the lives of the sweet little innocents. No longer will political affiliations be greater than the love of the babies. Each child will be seen as a treasure of heaven sent to Earth, not as an object which can be destroyed by those on Earth. It will also become obvious that in destroying a baby inside or outside of the womb is a rejection of the Holy Child of Bethlehem, whom Herod in his worldly ways tried to kill. This Christmas is a time to once more find in the love of the baby Jesus a true love for all babies seeing in each one of them Jesus as a baby and treasuring each one as you treasure Him.

Do Not Fear Persecution

Mar 7, 2009

MANY CATHOLICS are concerned over the anti-Christian stances of governments, politicians and organisations which promote opposing lifestyles to that which Christians try to live.

A growing intolerance by those who claim to be tolerant is raising its ugly head. Those who call for freedom of speech often only want that free speech if it agrees with what they say. Those who speak out against the wrongs promoted openly in the world today are attacked in an effort to silence them and are called bigots, narrow minded, homophobic etc. and maybe are threatened with legal action if they will not stop professing the truth of their faith.

When Christians speak out against same sex marriages because they understand the sacredness of marriage, it is claimed that they are trying to deny the rights of homosexuals but what is forgotten is that it is not a right that homosexuals can marry it is a grievous wrong. Marriage is between a man and a woman. NO ONE else.

When Christians object to children being adopted by same sex couples some say they are heartless and are denying those who cannot have children the opportunity to have a family. The child of course is forgotten and so are the bad moral and spiritual effects that will be placed upon the child by being put in such an abnormal situation. The institutions that refuse to give children for adoption to same sex couples are given the choice by some governments to obey or to close their adoption agencies.

When a Catholic speaks out against abortion they may be painted as extremists or people who are ignorant to the truth of when life begins. The rights of the woman become the only consideration and the rights of the baby are completely ignored and no one has the right, according to some, to say anything different. Christian hospitals may be forced to either perform abortions against their faith belief or face legal consequences. Health workers who oppose abortion may have their right of a conscience taken from them and forced to perform or assist with abortions or forced to recommend abortions. The freedom of the Christian to believe is ignored or denied.

When a Christian speaks out against fetal stem cell use they are sometimes looked upon as those who do not care about people with serious diseases that may be helped by the stem cells. Of course what is denied is the fact that babies are being killed so that it might help someone overcome an illness and that it is those who love Christ that are defending the innocents who cannot defend themselves.

When Christians speak of abstinence they are mocked and thought of those who are not living in the real world. Those who want to save themselves for marriage are often ridiculed. Yet, promiscuity is promoted openly as a natural and good expression of a person's humanity and all the terrible consequences of it are ignored.

Christian schools in some countries are forced to accept programmes opposed to Christian belief. Prayer or religious symbols are frowned upon and may not be worn in some public schools.

Employees in some instances are forced not to wear crucifixes or crosses.

With all this and more happening many Christians naturally feel under attack. However, what should be remembered is that it is in times of persecution the Catholic Church grows in strength and the faithful come closer to God. Persecution has been with the Catholic Church from the beginning and it is to be expected.

All Catholics should in these times be asking the Holy Spirit for the grace to live and proclaim their faith unafraid of the consequences. It is in these times Catholics can show the depth of their love for God by refusing anything that is in opposition to the law of God and by placing God's law and God's love before that of the world.

We have been given a glorious opportunity by God to show that we can be like the early church which, regardless of what the world did, held firm to the love of Christ. If we do we can be sure that because of our actions the future will be one where many will find full lives in Christ because of us.

Let us not fear persecution instead let us stand tall holding our faith up as a beacon that will draw many to it and let us thank God for the opportunity to do so.

In Love

Apr 11, 2009

IN LOVE evil was defeated, in love death was overcome, in love The Lord rose from the dead.

In His passion, death and resurrection The Lord, Jesus, showed all what life as a follower of His is meant to be and what it can be. His followers are supposed to be examples to all others of this truth He exposed.

The truth that if a person continues to love, regardless of what evil may do to them, in and with Jesus they will be victorious over evil.

The truth that death is not to be feared as in Our Lord, Jesus, death is but the doorway to heaven. Death not a curse but truly a blessing for those who love God.

The truth that if we live a life of love as best we can in the way The Lord asks then each person can rise in Him to live in His eternal glory with The Father and The Holy Spirit.

The Easter message is the message of victorious love and it is the message each of The Lord Jesus' followers is meant to be sharing with all others unafraid of what the world may do to them.

When fear enters our hearts we should turn to The Lord and find strength in His enduring love, the strength to overcome our fears.

When we confront evil in life we should confront it in gentle love just as The Lord did. While at times it may seem that evil is insurmountable we should look to The Lord and see that it is His love that is insurmountable and with His love in us so are we.

When gentle love appears so weak, know in truth it is more powerful than all evil can throw at us when it is the gentle love that imitates Our Lord's love. Living in this way of Easter each day we can rise in Our Lord Jesus' divine glory and become the sacrificial lambs of love we are meant to be, lambs that truly follow Christ in bringing the truth of His love to all.

He is risen so let us arise in Him and change the world by His grace and love seen in our lives.

Yes, that is very Christian Aug 11, 2009

SOMETIMES, AS Catholics try to live their faith and stand up for what is right and truthful they are accused of not being very Christian.

It may be when a parent refuses to accept their children living in sin or living immoral lives and asks the children to stop their bad behaviour. The children may respond by saying it is not very Christian to oppose what they do and it is their life they can do what they want. The son or daughter may demand that the parents accept their behaviour.

Societies too, in some countries, promote that it is perfectly normal to lead promiscuous lives with many sexual partners and at times have sex education classes for the young that express that belief. Some sex education classes in schools teach children about contraception, sexual techniques and that heterosexuality is not the only choice to be made. In Holland on a recent visit we read of a programme on TV that had a young boy and a young girl masturbating suggesting to the young that rather than risk HIV with sexual intercourse they should masturbate and showed them how to do it! In the USA I heard of a programme where sex educators were suggesting to young people that to avoid HIV and STD's, instead of sexual intercourse they should perform oral sex.

When parents do not want these things taught to their children some see them as unreasonable and that they deny their children the rightful education all should have. The truth is, it is very Christian to oppose what is wrong and to stand against it.

It is very Christian to advise your offspring against doing

what is wrong and what may be harmful not only physically and mentally but spiritually too.

It is very Christian to reject what is wrong and to never accept sin.

WITH THE terrible sin of abortion those who are pro choice frequently say that it is not very Christian to ignore or not treat as the primary concern the mother and her predicament and her freedom to choose. That it is unchristian to try and force others to have children they do not want.

The truth is it is very Christian to stand against the slaughter of the innocents. Nothing justifies the killing of a child inside or outside of the womb, as happens in partial birth abortions or when babies are left to die after being born alive after botched abortions. Nothing makes acceptable the holocaust of the innocents that is taking place in the world today.

While at times there are very sad circumstances that some pregnant women find themselves in this is never the fault of the baby and it is not right that the baby should be sacrificed for the mother. A parent is meant to sacrifice for their child, this is a basic value implanted in all by God but destroyed in some by the world and self. It is a value society is meant to hold as well but often does not.

The very Christian thing, in this awful situation, is to stand firmly against the taking of life and to do all that is possible to help those involved in this to see the error of their ways.

The very Christian thing to do would be to help the mother and the child and to work for society to do the same so that no woman would find themselves feeling so confused, or so desperate, or so lost that they feel they have to have their own flesh and blood, their own child killed.

Some today foolishly believe the world is overpopulated and see the need to control population growth through contraception. If a Christian does not agree with this view they may be seen as stupid or accused of not being very Christian as they are not considering the poor and needy in the world who do not have enough to eat. It is claimed that they may not have enough to eat because there are too many people in the world and not enough food and so control of the birth rate is essential if we are to feed all.

- It is very Christian to defend the right of all to be parents and of all children to be born.
- It is very Christian not to accept the deceptions and misunderstandings that support the need for population control.
- It is very Christian to cry out there is enough food and resources for all if we just share as we are meant to.
- It is very Christian to say those in the third world have the right to have as many children as God will give to them and they so desire within natural family planning methods.
- It is very Christian to say regardless of how many people live on Earth the climate does not need to be changed for the worse if we would just make the effort to look after it.

There are those today who claim it is not being Christian to oppose the use of condoms to reduce the HIV infection rate. They claim to oppose condoms is to ensure the growth of HIV and to bring about the deaths of many from it. Yet the reverse is true for it is very Christian to oppose condoms. Condoms have done little if nothing at all to halt the spread of HIV. In countries where condoms are the main preventative measures, HIV is rampant and not being halted. Yet, in Uganda where abstinence and monogamy are the main preventative measures the rate of HIV infection is lower.

No Christian should accept the use of condoms for any reason as their prime action is to prevent life. Also, condoms promote promiscuity, they do not encourage people to be faithful to their spouse. Condoms bring a false security where some think they can carry on with many partners sexually and have no or little risk of acquiring HIV. How foolish it is that some would trust their life to the thin layer of latex that a condom is made of (there are various reports stating that condoms if used perfectly every time have a failure rate of 2–3 % and typically used have a failure rate between 12–15 %).

So it is very Christian to call for abstinence, fidelity and moral lives and to reject the use of condoms.

In the world today there has been a major change in the way homosexuality is seen. Many now see it as a valid sexual orientation that no one should oppose. Homosexuality is seen as an acceptable alternative to heterosexuality and promoted as such by some movements and governments. To oppose homosexuality is even considered as an attack on a person's rights and humanity and as a discrimination against others. To oppose homosexuality is seen by some as not very Christian for surely if two people love each other regardless of gender they should be allowed to have a sexual relationship.

To stand against homosexual marriage is called by some as not very Christian for how could you deny two people in love the right to marry? To refuse same sex couples the right to adopt is often declared as an attack on the equal rights of people.

Whether governments, movements or society do not agree it is very Christian to oppose what is wrong. Homosexuality is not a valid sexual orientation, it is not part of the normal sexual function of procreation. Homosexuality is wrong and must be opposed by those who love the truth. As a Christian a person has a duty not to accept what is wrong even if the whole world says it is right. It is a duty to reach out to those trapped in this lifestyle and help them find the beauty of true love as God created it to be. To help those who cannot overcome their homosexuality to remain celibate and to find joy in the love of God.

Homosexuality is not a normal state for people and it is not a true part of mankind's gift of sexuality from God. It is impossible for homosexuals to have a marriage in the eyes of God even if the world says it is a marriage.

It is very Christian to stand firm in these truths, to do anything less is certainly not Christian and is a rejection of the Holy Catholic and Apostolic Church teaching.
- It is very Christian to oppose adoption of children by same sex couples as the child would be put in a situation where it is exposed to immorality and sin and may be educated to accept these wrongs as right.
- It is to be remembered always that it is also very Christian never to discriminate against others for any reason.
- It is very Christian never to judge another or condemn them.
- It is very Christian to see the weaknesses and mistakes of others and pray for them to be overcome while of course remembering your own faults and weaknesses.
- It is very Christian to lead others gently to the true way of life without demanding or trying to force them to do so, seeing that everyone is loved by God no matter who they are or how they live and you should love everyone too. Seeing the gentle love of Christ for others and showing that same gentle love in the way you act with others, even those who do what is wrong.
- It is very Christian to want everyone to be treated with respect and to be treated equally but in that equality not accepting what is wrong.
- It is very Christian to expect and demand your governments protect and care for the needy, the poor, the vulnerable and those in unfortunate circumstances.
- It is very Christian to demand your governments protect life not destroy it.
- It is very Christian to expect that you too have the right to be respected and treated equally.

Catholicism under attack
Nov 29, 2009

As I reflect on our faith and how in the past many great saints went out to the world to share the love of Christ with the peoples of the world regardless of what may happen to them I am reminded that I and many Catholics do not do enough to share the love of Christ with others. There seems to be either a fear or apathy about spreading the faith or maybe it is part of a weakness of one's own faith that stops a person doing so.

Today we Catholics are blessed to have many opportunities before us where we can bring the love of Christ into the lives of others because so many today do not know Christ and His Divine love. However, instead of taking hold of these opportunities we so often do nothing and let them slip by and so may let a soul miss the opportunity of knowing the fullness of God's love in Christ, Our Lord.

Secularism is increasingly attacking Catholicism trying to draw people into believing in no God at all and only to believe in the here and now and what the world offers. In Europe, the European Court ruled Crucifixes should not be on display in Italian schools. In Switzerland the Church is controlled by the government and the lay people and not the priests or Bishops. Many tread very carefully so as not to offend Muslims but when it comes to Catholics governments, the media and people freely attack the Catholic Church with no regard to the people's belief or feelings. It seems because Catholics do not respond with violence or in anger but with a forgiving love that makes us easy targets for those who would not speak out against Islam because of fear. This makes these people no more than bullies attacking those who appear weak but avoiding offending those who would respond violently.

Some protestants openly attack Catholics and try to draw Catholics away from the truth of Christ into the acceptance of whatever is mans belief and not what Christ, Our Lord taught and asked of us. With the belief that anyone can interpret Holy Scripture it is easy for the protesting denominations to embrace homosexuality, gay marriage, contraception and female ministers and bishops.

Muslims openly attack both physically and with force of law the Catholic faith. In some Muslim countries it is an offence to wear a crucifix, to speak of Jesus, to celebrate Mass or to pray in a prayer group. Catholic Bishops, priests and religious are subjected to murder, rape and torture. I was in England several years ago in Bradford speaking in the Catholic Church. The church was surrounded by high walls with barbed wire on top. Security cameras and security gates had to be installed. This was because Muslims in the area attacked the priest several times and often try to damage the church and abuse people going into it. Their claim is that Bradford is a Muslim town and no Catholic church should be in the area even though the church has been there long before the Muslim population and England is a not a Muslim country. There also have been approaches to the council to close the church because it offends Muslims.

However, we Catholics should not despair as Christ is with us and it is in times of persecution that the Church is graced and strengthened by God who brings up people to boldly profess the faith to all.

Today we are all called by God to be these people, to be the saints who stand firmly but gently in the truth of Christ. It is through us God will show His loving power and touch many in the world with His Holy Spirit to convert their hearts to the full truth of God. We are called to live our faith openly so that all can see Christ in us. We are called to stand against all wrong so that the truth of God can be seen through us.

We are called to reach out to all in the name of Christ so that all can come to know His Divine love.

We are called to share without fear the faith we know and love as the true faith.

Let us be the ones who show the world that secularism and political correctness is the cause of so many of the world's wrongs.

Let us be the ones who reach out to our protesting brothers and sisters inviting them to the full truth of Christ.

Let us be the ones who take to our Muslim cousins the knowledge of the Divinity of Christ so that they can truly come to know the Trinitarian God of love and peace.

I encourage each person to begin today and to continue every day praying for Muslim hearts to be open to Christ, Our Lord. I hope each person would pray three Our Fathers for Muslims to know The Father and The Son and the Holy Spirit. Pray in love and in the desire that they come to know the love of Christ which leads people deep into the heart of The Father by the grace of The Holy Spirit. Ask all those you know to pray for them, ask your prayer groups, your friends...everyone. Let us create a mountain of loving prayer that reaches up to heaven in a chorus of love for our Muslim cousins. Please join me in this and persevere even when nothing seems to be happening as in time God will pour out the blessings needed to change hearts and souls and to open them to the full truth of God.

Defending the Church
Mar 26, 2010

IN THESE times the Church is coming under a furious assault on its holiness as some highlight a number of the sinful events that have happened within it. First of course we must admit that there have been terrible abuses within the Church which sometimes have been handled badly. However, even when handled badly the intent was never to let the abuse continue. While some times the Church did try to deal with the problems within the Church rather than inviting outside help this is not an evil thing but unfortunately bad judgement which did have serious consequences.

These consequences were borne heavily by the abused and every effort to help those affected should be made.

No one should be surprised at the intensity of the attacks on the Church and His Holiness Pope Benedict XVI this is to be expected. Those who oppose the Church will always use every means possible to try and destroy it and today highlighting and exaggerating claims of abuse are the weapons they use. Of course the Church will be hurt by these attacks but remember it will never be overcome. It is also obvious by the timing of these attacks that some are trying to disturb this, the holiest time for Christians, and to distract people from the celebrations of Our Lord's suffering, death and resurrection.

If we look at what is happening with a clear mind and not one influenced by the popular attacks a different understanding emerges.

The Pope of course has been trying to stop further abuse and trying to help the victims with his apologies, his removal of some priests and Bishops and by stating a zero tolerance for these shameful acts. The response by some is to attack the Pope with misrepresentations of the facts.

An instance is the priest who sadly abused deaf children in the U.S. Some call for the Pope to be removed as they claim he knew of it. The facts are that the Vatican was informed decades (20 years) after the event at which time the priest involved was dying. The priest had begged forgiveness and so Cardinal Ratzinger decided that it would serve no purpose to pursue this as it may cause more pain to those involved if their abuse was made public. The priest died some months later. I think any compassionate person in this situation would have done the same.

Another attack on the Pope was that his brother George, a priest (and a rector of a famous church choir) had slapped a choir boy in 1960 and this was called abuse. In those days it was the norm to use corporal punishment in schools and throughout society and it was not seen as abuse. (Immediately after a law came out not to apply corporal punishment, George Ratzinger gladly consented and said, for him this new law was "a relief" Also, one of the former choir boys said they had respect and love for him, he wanted discipline but was like a grandfather for them, with a warm heart.) Should we now start actions against all schoolteachers or parents who physically punished children? To look back and impose today's values selectively on others is truly unjust.

In another attempt to hurt the Pope it is claimed he did not respond correctly to a priest behaving badly in Munich where he was Archbishop at the time.

The priest was from another German diocese and was removed from that diocese. Consent was asked from Munich archdiocese to send the priest there for psychological therapy. Archbishop Ratzinger agreed the priest could come and was to stay in a presbytery. The then vicar general, without consulting Archbishop Ratzinger or asking his permission, decided that the priest should do parish work during his stay. The Archbishop left the diocese shortly afterwards and was not informed of this.

None of these attacks have truly any real substance to them in regard to the Pope but this does not stop the distortion of the facts by some. It should also be remembered that in society until recently abuse was often kept hidden from the public gaze as it was believed this was the best course of action to take. Families, victims, organisations both governmental and private did not want it known that abuse occurred and so swept it under the carpet. Why then should we expect that this way of thinking would not enter the Church as the Church is full of people who come from society?

Today many cast the first stone without thinking of their own mistakes or of the mistakes of society in general which they and their families past and present bear some responsibility for as part of society. How sad it is that the wonderful work the Church does worldwide is ignored. The largest charity in the world is the Catholic Church which feeds the poor, treats the sick and helps the needy in many countries. So many religious devote their lives to doing good often sacrificing for the love of others. How easily the world ignores the priests and religious who are murdered, tortured or raped as they go out to help those in need. The vast majority of priests who are good and serve mankind are forgotten while the very few priests who offend are highlighted for their wrongs.

(A German professor for forensic psychiatry, Prof. Hans-Ludwig Kröber from Berlin, did a statistic on child abuse. From 1995 till now, there have been 210 000 cases of child abuse in Germany reported to the police. This makes some 14 000 cases per year. The number of clergy involved in these is 94 in this period of 15 years. The professor states that the probability that men living in celibacy do such crimes is 36 times smaller than that of "normal" men.)

The Church will survive this feeding frenzy as some try to eat away its holiness and as it has in the past will come out of this difficult time a stronger Church. Let us not lose heart but instead stand firm in our faith responding to the assaults on the Church not only with a forgiving love but with a love that proclaims the truth and defends the Church in its time of trial.

Called to Forgive   Apr 3, 2010

IN THIS holy time we are reminded of the majesty, wonder and power of The Lord's merciful and forgiving love. We are reminded how in His divine sacrifice Our Lord, Jesus, cried out to the Father for the forgiveness of mankind and how through His merciful heart that forgiveness was poured out in His blood and water as it washed over the world.

The Lord offered and continues to offer His forgiveness to all people, even the worst of sinners, and this is a great message of Easter and of our Catholic faith. How sad it is that there are many Catholics who cannot or will not forgive. Some have forgotten forgiveness is an essential part of our faith and that we have to be prepared to forgive all people if we are truly to live as Christ, Our Lord, calls us to. If a person cannot or will not forgive then they truly cannot know Christ.

Unforgiveness is a barrier between not only people but between God and man, for some in not forgiving through anger may be drawn into sin through actions of revenge. If a person will not forgive they may hold onto bitterness, resentment and even hatred, all of which are rejections of Our Lord's teachings. Sometimes people cannot forgive because their pride has been hurt and not forgiving seems to soothe their hurt. Some do not forgive because in holding on to the wrongs others have done takes their focus away from their own wrongs. Surely a sign of pride is the sinner who cannot forgive the sinner. If we do not forgive we deny Christ full entry into our lives as we refuse to listen to His words. In not forgiving we say that while Christ may forgive all, I will not, or that maybe my judgement is better than Christ's. In not forgiving also we forget that we ask the Father to forgive us as we forgive others so if we do not forgive others how then can we expect forgiveness for ourselves from the Father?

Yes, it is true that many people have been hurt terribly by others, physically, mentally or emotionally. Yes, it is true that many have been taken advantage of unfairly. However, Christ surely knew this when He called us to forgive. He did not say forgive some but not others, He said to forgive all no matter what they have done. Our Lord, Who suffered more than any human can with His last words still called out in love, 'forgive them Father for they know not what they do'. He lived and died the words He spoke and then The Lord rose to show the power and truth of those words. Are we going to remain imprisoned in the tomb of unforgiveness, or are we with loving and forgiving hearts going to rise in Christ to the heights of holiness He calls us to? The choice is ours.

Atheism   Apr 18, 2010

THERE ARE many people around the world who profess to be atheists and denounce religion as nothing more than mere superstition that has caused most if not all of the world's problems.

On a recent trip to the USA I saw a former governor of one of the states there boldly proclaim that all wars are caused by religion. This is also a statement I have heard from many atheists.

No one challenged him on this, giving the appearance that what he said was fact. When in fact what he said is of course nonsense. A few examples to prove this;
- The wars between France and England were generally over sovereignty.
- The American war of independence began over taxes on tea.
- The American civil war was over slavery.
- The Napoleonic wars were about the control of territory and peoples.
- China-Russia war over territory.
- World War 1 caused by the assassination of the Austrian Archduke Ferdinand and his wife by Serbians terrorists of the Black Hand. Also by political alliances and the seeking of power.
- World War 2 National Socialist Party in Germany taking control and invading other countries (ie. Poland)
- Vietnam War fight against communists
- Korean War fight against communists

There are many more which can be mentioned which were not caused by religion. This does not mean religion has not caused wars but it is not the only reason for them and the two world wars were not over religion.

Atheism itself has played a large part in causing wars this fact is frequently ignored or denied by atheists.

Atheists proclaim that in an atheistic world things would be much better than in one that is influenced by religion but if we look it becomes clear this is not so;
- Under the Russian communists life was very hard for most with millions being killed.
- China under Mao had the enormous cost in lives and suffering because of his cultural revolution.
- Pol Pot and his ideal communist state in Cambodia again millions killed.
- Ho Chi Minh in Vietnam.
- Kim of North Korea.

All these atheistic states have things in common; the people had or have little freedom, many were or are tortured and killed, many without food and many imprisoned for not following the party line. The little religion allowed was or is controlled by the state to suit its own purposes. These are the fruits of atheism.

I also remember recently hearing Richard Dawkins a well known atheist stating that the only reason people believe in God is because they were taught by their parents when they were young and brainwashed into believing in God. That the children believed because their parents had told them so and just like the story of Santa Claus they believed the story of Jesus. However, he ignored the fact that as children get older they realise the truth of Santa Claus and that the story is make-believe that he comes down the chimney with gifts etc. Yet, many as they grow older with the same wisdom keep their belief in God and realize in their own mind, heart and soul that God is real. They keep their belief because of personal faith and experience not because of what they were told.

Also, Dawkins' statements totally ignore countries like

Russia where the communist atheist state had control for 70 years. The communist state persecuted religion, banned religion, killing, imprisoning and re-educating believers. It did allow the Orthodox Church some limited activity which was controlled by the state but this was not widespread freedom of religion. In school and at home it was forbidden to discuss or teach religion. However, after 70 years of this as Russia emerged from communism many of the people embraced Christianity. The Orthodox Church (and the Catholic Church to a lesser extent) in Russia has grown enormously with many people attending church. Even the President and Prime Minister of Russia attend Orthodox Liturgy.

Recently at a university in Russia Prime Minister Vladimir Putin encouraged students to try to live the way of St. Francis of Assisi.

At a football match during Easter time (April 5th, Moscow Lokomotiv Stadium) one part of the crowd of thousands in the stadium were shouting, 'Christ is risen' and the other group of thousands answering, 'Truly He is risen.'

How then can Dawkins' statements be valid if people, most of whom have not been taught about God or encouraged to believe in God, freely embrace God?

How is it possible that people who were encouraged to deny God and to accept the communist atheistic way as the sole truth, change to embrace God in such large numbers?

Atheism has brought little good into the world but certainly has contributed to the decline of societies and morals. The Atheists tell others there is no God, enjoy life, to live for the here and now. As if a person cannot enjoy life because they believe in God. What rubbish! Their call to enjoy life is a call to selfishness as it is espoused do what you like as long as it does not hurt anyone. However, if wrong ways are embraced they always hurt someone. Sometimes the person themselves, as in what they do they may degrade their own body or the bodies of others, they lose respect for self or for others, they lose feelings of true love. Atheists often say the person can decide for themselves what is right or wrong or society can decide. How foolish this is because right or wrong does not depend on what a person or a society believes but is a constant that never changes. If people can decide what is right or wrong then these values change with the wind as public and personal opinions change. What is right today can become what is wrong tomorrow or vice versa.

History is full of examples where people or society has decided what is right or wrong and the terrible costs of this.

Atheists talk of tolerance but often are the most intolerant as they ridicule, abuse and attack those who believe in God. I have had atheists demand I prove there is a God well in response I demand atheists prove to me there is not a God.

Some atheists expect religion not to be taught in school or at home but expect their atheistic values to be regardless of what the people may want.

Atheistic governments and leaders sometimes force God loving people to abide by laws which oppose God's laws or teachings. Clearly seen in some communist states and dictatorships where imprisoning and even killing those who will not accept their atheistic decrees is common place.

While Christians must never deny those who do not believe in God the right not to believe, Christians must never accept the atheistic ways that go against what is Jesus' way.

Christians must never accept the changes to society that obviously hurt people through the degradation of morals and the degradation of true respect for one another.

Christians must never deny their Lord by denying their faith and must stand up firmly but gently and lovingly proclaiming Jesus as Lord to the whole world regardless of the cost.

The Other Side of the Coin

IT IS a difficult time for the Catholic Church as allegations of sexual abuse within the church are revealed. Those religious who are guilty of sexual abuse should be and are being called to account for their terrible crimes against the young. Truly paedophilia can never be justified and should always be condemned and those guilty of it rightly must face the full force of the law.

However, there is also a high price being paid by some priests who are falsely accused but this draws little attention from the media or the public. Often as soon as an allegation is made some believe it to be true and hold onto this belief regardless of the facts. The media at times seems to have the attitude of never let the facts get in the way of a good story. Some have their own agenda in attacking the church even using distortions of the truth to do so.

Recently I was in a country where on the news one of the major stories was about a priest accused of abusing two young people. The news story went into great depth explaining the allegations making it appear as if the priest was guilty. At the end of the story there was just a short sentence saying that one of the young people had withdrawn the allegation and that the court found that the priest had no case to answer in the other. Yet listening to the news story a person would be left with the impression the priest was guilty.

Where I live in Australia a wonderful old Irish priest was accused of sexually abusing a young person. The police launched an investigation and the priest was treated by the media as if he was guilty. The parents of the young person stated that the priest could not have done the alleged events as at the times they were supposed to have happened their teenage child was with them. The young person was also known to have some other problems in life. The priest had his ministry restricted during the long investigation and was very upset that he could not freely perform his duties. These accusations bore heavily upon the priest causing him a large amount of stress. After some time the allegations were found to be untrue, as many knew they would be. About three months later the priest died. Some, like I, believe it was from the stress he was put under.

In another country a very well known priest with a high profile including appearing often on television was accused of molesting a young man. The priest denied it but was removed from public duties only being allowed to say mass in private as investigations got underway. All the work he was doing which was bringing many to the church or to a stronger faith came to a halt. Over a period of many years in three different courts the priest was found innocent of the charges. After such a long time his priesthood has been damaged severely and he has been tarnished unfairly. The good work he was doing has ended.

These are just three of many cases I know of where the priest was innocent but because of false allegations they have had their ministry destroyed or brought to a standstill.

I do not hear the media apologising for or correcting their unbalanced reports when a priest is found innocent. Some of the media and those who dislike the Catholic Church highlight even accusations that obviously have no foundation so as to hurt the church. Often they judge before a court has.

Listening at times to the news or reading some newspapers people would get the impression that the church is full of paedophiles and that the church actively hides or protects them. Little is said about how the Catholic Church in comparison to other organisations has a low rate of sexual abuse of minors. So little is said about the openness of the church in these matters, an openness which rightly has some protection for those who are not yet proven guilty of anything.

Isn't the right of those who are not yet proven to have committed a crime to be considered innocent until proven guilty? Sadly this does not seem to apply to the priests as any allegation against a priest seems to be enough for many. Of course if there are allegations of sexual abuse a priest should be placed under strict controls until the truth, whatever it is, comes to light but he should also not be at the mercy of the lynch mob in the media until the truth is known.

Does not each person deserve a fair trial where the facts are presented and the judges or juries decide the truth? I expect most people would want that for themselves or their loved ones if they were accused. Shouldn't it be the same for all?

Paedophilia is terrible crime that is one of the scourges of society. Sadly it happens in all walks of life and it seems to be a cancer of society that is hard to eradicate. We must pray for this evil to be destroyed and pray that it is done in the right way, so that no innocents are hurt whether they be young or old, the abused or the accused.

Let us pray for true justice.

I also encourage that each person adopts a priest in prayer and prays daily for their priesthood to be good, holy and strong.

On Prayer   Aug 27, 2010

DEAR FATHER ...

You asked me yesterday about what I do to avoid distractions in prayer and I replied I ask the Holy Spirit to help me pray and avoid distractions.

I should have also said that I still get distracted but that The Lord told me not to give up or get frustrated with prayer because I am distracted. Instead to realize that through persevering in prayer even though it may be difficult your perseverance in itself is a prayer of love and a sign of your love for God.

Also that I should see the distractions as little crosses that

I am asked to carry and when I accept to carry them they can become doorways of grace for me and for others.

I should also understand that the distractions are often placed there by evil to stop me praying, even when I am drawn in to simple thoughts of life these thoughts are encouraged by evil so as to stop me thinking of God.

So prayer is a battle where each person confronts evil even though they may not realize this. It is a battle we can win by the grace of God by asking the Holy Spirit for the grace to persevere and to not get drawn into thoughts of self pity, disappointment or frustration when we are distracted.

Instead to offer those distractions themselves as a prayer of love to God and know even the prayer full of distractions is still a sign of your love for God because you have made the effort to pray and in love persevere in prayer.

God bless,
Alan Ames

The Acceptance of Sin

Sep 6, 2010

HAVING LIVED an extremely sinful life myself I have some awareness of how people so easily can accept sin or what is obviously wrong in life. We are bombarded with sin in what we watch, what we read and what we hear from others. In this environment people can become more open to sin and to be led into believing what is wrong is right. It is like a subtle and sometimes not so subtle brainwashing.

Self interest groups promote their own agenda which maybe at first most would disagree with but as time goes on and more publicity and attention is given to these agendas the public opinion can and so often is changed. What in the past would have been rejected by most can so easily become accepted as normal and right by many. The voices that stand up for true values then are seen as the extremists and may be ridiculed, demonised or even prosecuted for their holding on to what is right. Society now decides what is morally correct and what is not regardless of the truth. Those who disagree with society's moral view can become villains in the eyes of some.

I am amazed as my life unfolds how I see people so easily led, how the majority can be manipulated by the few to suit their own ends. There are similarities in the way people are led usually a good thing that many would support is promoted by an interest group but hidden underneath this is the other agenda.

The major environmental party is an example. Most people agree that the planet, the animals, the trees and the environment around us needs to be respected and taken care of, so in these areas many would have sympathy with the major environmental party. However, who looks beyond this to see the other agenda? Euthanasia, gay marriage, abortion, legalization of drugs, these are just some of the hidden bad. If the environmental party stood up and proclaimed their true and full agenda I am sure many who support them would not. Of course it is not only this party and their leaders who do this but many other political and public groups also. It seems to be the common practice to tell the people the good they want to hear to get support but hide the bad away from them. Then as some of these groups get influence slowly but surely they start using their positions to change public opinion so as to accept what in the beginning would never have been accepted by society.

It saddens me to see how in many countries morals have almost collapsed and sin reigns in a great number of lives. One of the shames of the modern world is how parents now teach their children few if any morals and so a large number of the new generation grow up not knowing what is right or wrong. It is becoming an immoral and an amoral world. The price of this is that so many are lost in life. So many cannot find true love for they do not know what true love is. What hope for the young is there in knowing how to have a full and proper relationship when a person running for the prime ministership of one country is living with her partner in a de facto relationship and not married to him? What sort of example does that set? Yet many in that country have voted for this person. Are we blind to sin or do we just do not care anymore?

As a Catholic I am particularly unhappy with the political and society leaders who profess to be Catholic yet support and promote that which is anti-Catholic. These people do not seem to understand by their words and actions that they may be leading others into sin and away from God. I have heard some declare that they are strong Catholics but that they support abortion, gay marriage, same sex relationship adoption, condoms and drugs of addiction legalization. Do they not understand that in accepting and supporting these wrongs they deny their faith and their God?

Today the world sinks into the confusion and suffering that sin brings. Many lives are hurt, destroyed or devalued. Many do not know the true happiness of life and struggle along not knowing what is wrong with the world and why. Now is the time for all those who love God and truly try to live as He asks to stand up and profess their faith openly and unafraid. Now is the time for the light of Christ, Our Lord, in our hearts to illuminate the dark. Now is the time to say enough is enough.

How do we do this? We do it by being the examples of love and compassion that Jesus, The Lord, calls us to be. We do it by standing firmly in the truth at all times and never accepting sin or the wrongs that society may try to force upon us. We do it by gently reaching out to all explaining the truth of God and of life to them. We do it by being the people who imitate the early church where so many stood for Christ, Our Lord, no matter what the cost. Let us be the ones who stop the advance of evil and it's immorality in the world by living the moral life we were created to live and letting all know that we do and why.

May God strengthen us all with the grace we need to truly be His Son, Jesus' followers.

Christmas Message Dec 16, 2010

IN THIS most joyful season of the celebration of the birth of The Lord, Jesus, we are presented with the great opportunity of spreading His love joyfully by reminding everyone what this time truly means. Today for some Christmas is no more than a holiday, a break from work to spend with family or friends or a time to party. Others see it as a time to shop and a time to give and receive presents. Some businesses see Christmas as nothing more than the chance to sell more and to make more profits.

However, we as followers and lovers of Christ, Our Lord, have a duty to let all see and hear the true meaning of Christmas. Sadly many of us do not fulfil our duty as so often we get drawn into the worldly and secular ways of the time instead of revealing in the spiritual ways of this glorious celebration of divine love. We shop, we party, we enjoy family, we relax, we socialize and yet so often we only give The Lord little thought, we pay Him scant attention. Yes, we may send Christmas cards, go to carol services and to the Christmas Mass but for many that is it. The Christ child is put aside as we think we have done our duty, we have paid our respects, we believe we have done enough.

It is interesting that many Christians complain about the commercialization of Christmas. Complain about Christmas being changed by society to be just another holiday. Yet, that is what so many of us make it. Can we expect any different if we do not behave in a different way than others? How can Christians call for Christmas to be respected if in truth many do not do this themselves? If those who love Christ, The Lord, superficially celebrate Christmas, how can we expect others to find the truth of the birth of baby Jesus?

This Christmas and every Christmas let us first and foremost think of the great gift of love that God gave to mankind in His only Son, Jesus. Let us think of how we can bring Jesus to others in joyful love, for this is how Jesus came to earth; in joyful love. Let us reach out to everyone we meet with a loving heart and truly say, "Merry Christmas" and "God bless you". Not just saying the words but praying them from within the depths of our souls. Let us ask God to give each one of us the opportunities to spread His love to those we come in contact with.

Let us not be afraid to call out joyfully that The Lord has come and that He has come in love to save all mankind. Let us even to those who deny Christmas and Christ, Our Lord, offer God's blessings to them in our prayerful words. Let us be the ones to lead others to the Holy Child of Bethlehem so that in Him they may find holiness. Let us not be afraid and cower in fear of ridicule or rejection. Instead let us stand tall in love and joyfully proclaim to the world that this is the time to remember the greatest gift that has and ever will be given to mankind, God's only Son, Jesus.

Protestant Discussions

Mar 7, 2010

DURING MY travels I encounter many people of the protesting denominations and always I am glad to do so.

Often I see in our protestant brothers and sisters a strong desire to love God and to help others. I see in them the desire to know and live to the word of God and their knowledge of Holy Scripture, as it is presented to them, is usually very good.

I see in our protestant friends a ground that has already been partially prepared for the fullness of truth and needs only to be sown with the complete truth of Our Lord and saviour, Jesus Christ.

In the many discussions I have with them it becomes clear that the majority are good people who just have been confused a little and need the clarity of the full truth brought into their lives.

When I speak of the full truth I mean of course the truth of the Holy Word of God as found in the Holy Bible that has not been altered or adulterated by man to suit their own understanding or own agenda. We must remember that there are many changes made in the protestant bibles, I remember several years ago when a new edition became available it was stated that there were more than 20 000 changes within it! This all stems from back to the times of Luther and then Tyndale who produced the English Bible. So it is clear that even though many protestants can quote Holy Scripture the scripture they quote is often not exactly what was given to mankind. It seems also that many change the meaning of scripture to suit self. This is in line with the early protestant founders who declared that anyone can decide what scripture means. With this belief it is therefore easy to manipulate the Word of God to suit ones own desires. Of course it is not only protestants that do this, some Catholics do so also, the difference is that it is acceptable to do so within the protesting denominations.

With this manipulation of scripture many can so easily deny what The Lord actually said. Here is an example of a conversation I recently had and is similar to those I often have with protestants:

Protestant: *'Why do you believe there is only one church given by Jesus. Surely there can be many and we are all equally valid?'*
    Reply: 'Well The Lord said in Holy Scripture there is only one flock that He is shepherd of and St. Paul also said there should be no division that we all should be united as one in Christ.'

Protestant: *'How do you know you are the right flock and we are not?'*
    Reply: 'It is clear through Holy Scripture and through the history of Christianity that the One Holy Catholic and Apostolic Church is the one Christ gave to man. He founded the Church on St. Peter the rock when He said, "You are Peter and upon this rock I shall build my Church." Note He said Church not churches.'

Protestant: *'That was only for those times not now and it was only Peter He said it about and Peter is no longer is here.'*
    Reply: 'When did The Lord say it was only for those times? Also Jesus said to St. Peter "What you bind on Earth is bound in Heaven and what you loose on Earth is loosed in Heaven." When St. Peter passed his authority on to the next Pope that is bound in Heaven regardless of what people say. This is a Divine decree. So the next Pope and all who have followed him in the chair of Peter have had this authority passed on to them and also have the power to bind and loose on Earth and in Heaven and become the rock upon which the Church is built.'

Protestant: *'It was only symbolic, it was not meant to be taken literally.'*

Reply: 'But you say you live to the Word of God and now you say His word is only symbolic. Why live to it then? Where did The Lord say it was symbolic? He was very clear about this statement even saying the gates of hell could not stand against the Church He founded with St. Peter as the rock it is built upon. He also in a parable in Matthew 7 spoke of building the house on a rock and how it did not collapse because it had been built solidly on the rock and stated, "Anyone who listens to these words of mine and does not act on them will be like a fool who built his house on sand." Here The Lord is saying very clearly build your house, the church, on the rock which he has told us is St. Peter and not on the shifting sands of the opinions of people who decide they know best.'

Protestant: *'No He did not mean that. He also said where two or three are gathered in His name He is with them. In our church we pray and He is with us and we prophesy, pray for deliverance in the name of Jesus. There are healings when our pastor prays for them. Jesus is with us. You are wrong.'*

Reply: 'Yes, He is with any who gather to pray in His name but that does not make those people part of His Church. If people pray to The Lord but refuse to live to the fullness of what He asks of us they by their choice place themselves outside of His Church. When you pray, yes He is there, but He is there trying to lead you to the fullness of truth and not leave you in a partial truth.'

Protestant: *'Why then does He work miracles among us? Surely this shows we are right?'*

Reply: 'Of course He will work miracles. The Lord wants to help everyone in life and if miracles are needed for people He will provide them. However, this does not mean these signs validate your denomination. In Holy Scripture, again in

Matthew 7 The Lord explained about the true disciple, "Not everyone who says 'Lord, Lord,' will enter the kingdom of heaven, but only the one who does the will of My Father in heaven. Many will say to me on that day, 'Lord, Lord, did we not prophesy in your name? Did we not drive out demons in your name? Did we not do mighty deeds in your name?' Then I will declare to them solemnly, 'I never knew you. Depart from Me, you evildoers.'" The will of the Father is that people follow all His Son Jesus asks of us and not what they decide is worth believing in or not.'

Protestant: *'But you Catholics do not do the Father's will that is why there was the reformation. It was through the reformation the true way was found.'*

Reply: 'Yes, there have been mistakes in the Catholic Church and there will be mistakes in the future I am sure. Those mistakes however were made by either sinful people or by confused people. This however does not change the fact there is one true church, the church built on the rock of St. Peter, the church full of sinners trying to live to God's way.'

Protestant: *'That is why the reformation was so important, it put the mistakes right. So it is only the reformed churches that are valid now.'*

Reply: 'How can that be when those who formed the protesting denominations were men and the One who founded the Holy Catholic and Apostolic Church was Christ Himself? Also the reformed denominations were founded by very confused men. Did you know that Luther stated it was alright to commit murder a 100 times a day or rape 100 times a day as long as you cling to Christ?'

Protestant: *'That is not true.'*
    Reply: 'Yes it is. It is in a letter written by Luther called, 'Let your sins be strong' and yet Jesus told us not to sin so Luther goes against the Word of God.'

Protestant: *'You are lying.'*
    Reply: 'Look it up for yourself.'

Protestant: *'You are a liar. I do not believe you.'*
    Reply: 'Then look it up and see for yourself.'

Protestant: *'No, I do not believe you.'*
    Reply: 'How about Calvin who said that people are predestined to either go to Heaven or Hell. (The words of Calvin; Predestination we call the eternal decree of God, by which He hath determined in Himself what He would have to become of every individual of mankind. For they are not all created with a similar destiny; but eternal life is foreordained for some, and eternal damnation for others.)
    'If that is the case why should anyone live to Jesus' way if it is already decided where you are going. Also if it does not matter what you do in life you are already predestined, that means a person can commit as many sins as they like and it does not change where they are going. If there is predestination why was the sacrifice of The Lord needed for sinners? Why did The Lord call people to repent and not to sin again? Why did The Lord come to Earth? All this would not be necessary?'

Protestant: *'You do not know what you are talking about.'*
    Reply: 'Find out for yourself. Read about the lives of Luther and Calvin and Henry the Eighth and see how they lived and what they actually said. You might be surprised.'

Protestant: *'No I do not believe you. You Catholics are all the same.'*
    Reply: 'That is your choice but I suggest you actually learn about what you believe by researching the history of your faith.'

I LEFT the discussion shortly after this point but hoped and prayed this protestant woman would investigate what I had said trusting in God that He would lead her to His full truth and love.

I encourage all Catholics not to be afraid to engage protestants in discussions of faith, for even though many protestants can quote scripture verbatim, often their understanding and their quotes are built on sand. Catholics have the firm foundation of the rock of St. Peter and should stand unwavering on that rock.

Catholics should know their faith and be unafraid to share it. Yes, it may be difficult at times but if a seed of truth can be planted then a great harvest may come from that. Even if you leave not certain you have achieved anything trust in God that the words you said in gentle love will bear fruit.

Be gentle in your way but firm in the truth. Be understanding in your words without ever denying the truth of Catholicism. Importantly, always ask the Holy Spirit to give you the grace and gifts you need to truly seed this fertile ground with the full truth of God's love in His Son, Jesus, and in the one true Church He gave to mankind...the One Holy Catholic and Apostolic Church.

THE BOOK 'What is truth,' is an ideal tool to use when evangelizing protestants because it has many of the historical statements by Luther and other founders of the reformation and clearly shows how their words at times opposed the statements of Christ Himself.

No More Than Our Duty
Apr 23, 2011

HE IS risen from the grave! Let all those who truly love The Lord, Jesus, rise up in love and proclaim to the world this divine truth. This is what The Lord asked the apostles to do and it is the same that He asks us to do. Let us go out to the world each day of our lives and share in our words and actions the truth of Easter and the joyful love this divine truth brings to life.

With so much misery in the world today people, regardless if they understand it or not, need to hear of the eternal love of The Lord, Jesus, and the eternal life He offers to all in His love.

With so much suffering in the world today people should know The Lord, Jesus suffered for them and shares in their suffering. That The Lord, Jesus is there to help and comfort people in their painful times, that He will give people the grace and strength needed to endure anything and that, yes, when it is for the best He will lift the crosses from the shoulders of people.

With so many in need in the world today people should be reminded in The Lord, Jesus, is all they need. Those with plenty should be reminded that The Lord, Jesus calls them to share in love with the needy. Reminded that this is a duty that brings us to imitate Christ in His total giving of self for those in need; a duty that needs to be fulfilled.

With so many troubled hearts in the world today the peace of Christ should be proclaimed to all people. The peace that never left Him through His suffering and that will remain in the hearts of those who embrace Christ in love.

- The peace that soothes the troubled heart.
- The peace that brings an end to conflicts.
- The peace that mankind was created to live in.
- The peace all should know and experience.

With so many lives lost in darkness and sin the light of Christ has to be shone upon those who are lost along the way so that they can find the right path to walk in life. We, the followers of

The Lord, Jesus, are meant to be the vessels of His Divine Light that illuminate the darkest recesses. We are called to be beacons of love leading others to a resurrected life in Christ, Our Lord.

There is a world out there waiting to hear the full truth of our resurrected Lord and we are called to be the heralds of the good news of God's eternal love in His risen Son, Jesus.

Let us rise up in love and be the bringers of the eternal light of salvation to all, unconcerned of what the world may think of us, may say about us, and may do to us. As true followers of Christ, Our Lord, it is our duty to declare His glorious love to all and to share the way to heaven in Him with all. Let us not remain trapped in the tomb by our fears, selfishness or pride. In humble love of God and of others let us put self aside and go out fearlessly to proclaim the love of Christ to all by the way we live, by the way we love and by sharing our lives and love with others as the people who have died in Christ and have been resurrected in Him as the people of love.

The Standard of Christ   Jun 2, 2011

DEAR FRIENDS in Christ,

Looking around the world today we can see there is much suffering and pain. So many unhappy people, people who are confused, people who are lost in life and people who are empty within. In all of this we should not despair, in all of this we should not lose hope and in all of this we should not fear. It is easy to be drawn into thoughts and feelings of hopelessness and into apathy believing there is nothing to be done and so accept the state of the world as that is the way things are there is nothing I can do.

The media places before us daily in the news such sadness, suffering and evil that a wearing down effect seems to occur where people become almost numb to what is happening and no longer care about the plight of others. The deceptions of those in power decay people's trust in others. As people start to lose hope, trust and caring about others hearts become closed to God and opened to darkness. This darkness is enveloping the world and few recognize this.

We however as followers of The Lord, Jesus, should not lose heart. We should recognize that God calls us to be lights of His joyful love that bring hope to all. Disciples that bring the glorious truth of Jesus to all, knowing that in doing so, by God's grace, we can change lives and yes, even change the world for the better. We can be the ones who help people to trust in Jesus, Our Lord, by showing people they can trust in us. We are here to lift others up to The Lord in love so that the confusion clears, the emptiness is filled and the lost find their way in Him. For this to happen the followers of The Lord, must themselves be the breath of truth that blows away the deceits of the world. We must show people the good in the world by letting them see the good of God in us. Sadly some Catholics do not do this as they themselves have been led to despair over the state of the world. Some fear the world will end and spend more time focusing on that than on sharing the love of Our Lord, Jesus. Our faith calls us not to despair, not to fear and not to worry about self but to be like Christ. To be lights in the dark, to bring hope where there is none, to bring happiness to the unhappy, to replace fear with trust in God, to lift people out of despair and up to The Lord, to fill empty lives with the love of God.

Let not people look at Catholics and say they are people just like us. Let them say here are fearless, joyful, loving people who I want to be like. Let us set the standard for Christ in the World, the standard that attracts all to Christ so that all can be at peace in Him and find salvation in His Divine love.

The Seal That Cannot Be Broken   Jul 26, 2011

THERE ARE politicians in Australia and Ireland calling for priests to be forced by law to break the confessional seal. This is in response to the shocking and terrible crimes of child abuse and some cover-ups of it within the Church.

While it is right and proper that anyone guilty of these crimes against man and God should face justice and receive the punishment they deserve it is not right to try and enforce the breaking of the confessional seal.

The sanctity of the confessional is a vow between a priest and God, which for no reason, no matter how vile, cannot be broken. Since the beginning of the Church under many different empires and ideologies priests have kept this sacred vow some even giving their lives for it. Fascism, communism, dictatorships, secular and non – Catholic groups have been unable to force or persuade priests and the Church to break this vow and if politicians today think they can do it then truly they do not know Catholicism and its history which has many a brave priest holding firm to their promise to God. This vow before God is greater than the human vows doctors take in refusing to make medical matters such as HIV status of patients available to others or lawyers refusing to make known their clients admissions to crimes.

For me the sadness is that there is a silence from many Catholics on this matter. Some even believe that the politicians are right. This shows there are those who do not know their faith or some who do not care about the sacred truths of their faith. It is not surprising with so few Catholics going to the sacrament of reconciliation that there is not a great outcry against these politicians. People should see this for what it is, an attack on the faith, and should stand up and defend the Holy Catholic faith. That does not mean ignoring the offenses against the young committed or the at times inadequate responses. Surely we should expect and demand that the Church protects the young and reports anyone guilty of such abhorrent sins. We also should expect the Church to keep its sacred vows to God including the seal of confession. If the Church accepted what these politicians are calling for who would go to confession? Who would trust a priest with their most personal matters? If the confessional seal could be broken for this over time the governments could demand more and more sins should be reported. Authoritarian regimes could use it to spy on and control the people.

Our faith would be weakened as who would truly confess their sins and in not doing so people would hold onto sin and the problems that come with it. Part of our relationship with God is to open our hearts and recognize our sins and weaknesses asking for His forgiveness and the grace to overcome our weaknesses. Because of our humanity it is often not possible to see the answers to our weaknesses by ourselves and so God through the priest gives the grace, advice and encouragement we need in the Holy Sacrament of Reconciliation. The divine grace received in a true confession is grace that forgives, heals, comforts and strengthens. It is also a grace that when fully accepted would lead a person to admit to the serious crimes they have done and face the consequences for them. What people also need to realise is that a priest can, and most likely would, withhold absolution in the case of a heinous crime until the person gives themselves up to the appropriate authorities.

Confession of sins is a pillar of the Catholic faith and all Catholics should stand up and defend this holy gift from God.

No Catholic should in any way support those who call for the breaking of the confessional seal as in doing so they support those who seek to weaken the faith. While the arguments for doing so may seem justified they are not. As Catholics we must put what is holy and sacred before what is the will of man even when man's will seems to be the answer to a problem.

Remember too that the Pope and the hierarchy of the Church are working hard to ensure these things do not happen again. Often the Church is presented as doing little or nothing or as being full of people trying to protect evil doers. This of course is not the truth as anyone who would take the time to read the guidelines for dealing with these matters would see. Yes there have been serious mistakes made but they were made by individuals not the Church. Listening to the media it would seem the Church is an evil empire and not the Holy Church that it truly is. We should consider who would want people to think this way and why and of course the prince of deceit springs to mind.

Let us stand up and be counted. Let us cry out for true justice and let us say firmly to the politicians, governments and the world that NEVER will we accept the confessional seal be broken.

A Warning   Oct 5, 2011

IT WAS in 1994 that God came into my life and lifted me out of the self-imposed prison of sin and worldliness. From the beginning as I began to meet people in my new life for God until today there has been a constant flow of information and messages about the end times that I hear from others. At first I was assured by many Catholics that the world was going to end or a warning would be given to mankind in 1998, it did not and was not. Then it was the year 2000; again nothing happened. Various dates since then have been given the most recent being 2012. This date is taken from the interpretation of an old Mayan calendar which predicts the year as 2012. Until now nothing has happened and I am confident 2012 will pass without the world ending. I certainly am looking beyond that in serving God on Earth if it is His will I do so.

How sad it is that so many Catholics are eager to hear of the end times and cling to the messages of doom that are spread around the world. As Catholics we should be clinging only to The Lord and hope for a better future in Him. We should be trusting in and believing in His words that NO ONE except The Father knows the time the world will end. If some one declares they know the time and date then they are rejecting and denying Christ's words. Some today are drawn into what goes against Christ's word, it seems as if they find some excitement in thoughts of the world ending and disasters happening. The disasters today are claimed by some as signs the end is near. Yet there have always been disasters, they are part of the history of mankind since we first sinned and they will continue until the end of time. Some live in fear that the world's end is near. However, we should have no fear and as Christ said we should stand tall and hold our heads high in His love waiting for His eternal embrace.

To me it seems this excitement people find in the end times or the fear some have of the end times shows that there is a weakness of faith. If a person lives a sacramental life and lives for Christ by completely embracing the One Holy, Catholic and Apostolic faith then there should be no room for fear or the need for this type of excitement. Living completely in the faith removes these fears. Living in and for the sacraments fills one with the excitement of God's love.

As a people who trust completely in God each one of us is meant to live each day as an example of Jesus, Our Lord. Jesus, who never showed fear. Jesus, who opened His heart to all so that each one could find security in His love. Jesus, in whom all the excitement we need can be found. How can we be an example to others if we are afraid? How can we be an example to others if we focus on the world ending? How can we show the heart of Christ to others if we believe in a Mayan pagan prophecy and ignore the words of Christ?

Some think that by telling people the world is about to end it will bring others back to God. People brought back by fear soon leave if they see nothing has happened or some prophecy did not come true. People brought back in and by love tend to stay. People who come back in love have a true faith. Whereas people who come back in fear often do so in self-interest and maybe with thoughts of self-preservation. What sort of faith is that?

As followers of Jesus Christ, The Lord, we should live each day as if this is our last day. We generally never know when our last breath will be taken. So instead of worrying about what may or may not happen in the future, we should be concerned about living today in the right way, for today may be the day we face Christ in death.

Remember Jesus Christ, Our Lord, calls each one of us to be a loving, joyful and fearless person. Let us be that way so in us others can see the peace of heart that Christ offers to all in His love.

I encourage all of you to live each day as if it is your last day, stop worrying about the future and take care of today. Live each day as a Catholic day and know if you do so eternal life with God is yours.

The Christmas Gift Dec 6, 2011

ONCE AGAIN the joyful time of our Saviour's birth is upon us and we are reminded of the great blessing of God coming to earth as man. With this magnificent act of humility and love God showed mankind that He is not a distant God but the one true God whose desire is to be with us not only in spirit but in flesh also. The Divine One exposed the depth of His love for mankind by sending His only Son so that mankind could come to know that truly we are the family of God and that mankind is truly loved by God. In that holy moment in Bethlehem mankind's saviour took His first breath and in doing so breathed a new beginning for mankind. In His divine breath was the renewing exhalation of God that came to blow away the old misunderstandings and replace them with the full truth of God's divine love. In the first heartbeat outside the womb that the Holy Child of Bethlehem had was nothing but love; love of His Father and love of mankind. With that heartbeat began a new relationship of love between God and man. Every heartbeat that followed in His Holy life was the same as the first one. For His heart never stopped loving and His heart never stopped showing how God treasured mankind's love.

As Our Divine Lord opened His eyes the first sight He saw was His mother Mary and He looked upon her in love. Then He looked to Joseph in love and saw in both of them how the love of mankind can be; pure and holy. In these two humans He saw how mankind was created to be. When His mother held Him in her arms close to her chest and rocked Him gently back and forth The Lord, Jesus, felt her love and felt the comfort of it. While at the same time she was filled with the joy of the divine love of God touching her.

Now The Lord, Jesus, looks to all of us with those same eyes that looked upon Joseph and Mary and He looks upon us with love. He looks and reaches out to each one with the same heart of love pouring out grace in abundance; grace that is there to lead mankind to Him through His blessed mother Mary. He calls mankind to welcome the embrace of His mother's comforting love and to unite in love with her and St. Joseph so that our hearts beat as one as we come to Him. He breathes out His Holy Spirit to draw all people into pure and holy lives as part of the Holy Family of God so that we can be close to Him and live joyfully in His love as we were created to do.

Once again this Christmas, God offers Himself to us as a gift of love in the giving of Himself in humility. We should not be blind to what is offered and we should also help others to understand the great gift of love that God bestowed on mankind. Not because it makes Him any greater but because it can make each one of us greater when we accept what is offered and truly become the Holy Family of God.

The Year Ahead
Jan 26, 2012

LET US all look ahead to the year before us in the hope that many will be blessed and find the true love of God in His only Son, Jesus. As it is only in His love that true peace in lives and on Earth can be found to it's fullest. It is only in His love that life can be complete. It is only in His love that the truth, gentleness, compassion that is meant to be part of lives can be discovered in the highest form. It is only in His love that the eternal bliss of divine love can be experienced. One of my prayers each day is that all people, not only those I know or who ask for prayers, will be touched and blessed by God so as to have a new life in Christ. I ask all of you to join me in this prayer (I am sure many of you are praying for this already) as the world today is a world with little love, hope, or compassion. So many people know little happiness and live in despair. So many do not know the love of God and so many do not know love at all. If we unite in prayer then the grace Our Lord, Jesus, pours out through our prayers will change the lives of others. It is important we persevere and know that even when we do not see or understand it God's grace is working and people are changing. I thank you for all your prayers for me and ask you to pray for those in the world who are more deserving than I am; the poor, the needy, those who do not know God or His Son, Jesus, and those who are lost in the dark.

Conscience and Faith
Feb 13, 2012

IN RECENT times certain governments try to force Catholics to deny their faith and beliefs and to go against their consciences. Our faith cannot be subject to the will of a government as then it would be nothing more than secularism cloaked in the name of faith. Also, when the governments change then could come a change of faith.

Our Catholic faith is supposed to be a relationship of love between God and man. A relationship where people try their best to live as Our Lord, Jesus, calls us to. A relationship that puts God before all else and above all else where we are obedient to His holy will in all things. With the eyes of heavenly love that come with trying to live as Catholics, a rejection of the world's ways that oppose the will of God, is born within us and grows within us as we seek to live for God.

Our conscience guides us by the grace of God to know what is right and what is wrong. Our conscience is an expression of our soul's desire to be close to God and filled with His divine love. Our conscience works to keep us on the right path and to avoid error and sin. Our conscience is a treasure of grace but sadly we do not always listen to it and listen to the graceless, and what seems to be the clever, arguments of the world instead.

It is our conscience that exposes who we truly are, the person we are and if we listen to it helps us know who we are. It is a great blessing from God that we have this within us; a blessing that all have but not all respect. In the history of the church so many have given every thing to live to the conscience bestowed upon them by God. Many have made the ultimate sacrifice so as to keep faith with God and their conscience. Communism, fascism, dictatorships and religions that say 'convert or die' have been unable to overcome the true believers and their relationship of love with the one true God, The Holy Trinity. Rivers of holy martyrs blood have been shed in the love of Our Lord, Jesus, and the faith He gave to us; rivers that wash over the world soaking it in the sacrificial love of God.

Today, secularist, socialist and sinful leaders try to force Catholics to deny their faith and their conscience. It is done with a smile and the arguments that it benefits people if Christians would give up their faith, give up the morals by which they are called by God to live to. If Christians accept these arguments and bow to the will of their leaders the world becomes worse not better. A person cannot be a Christian and follow the world instead of following Christ.

It is by following the will of Christ, that each individual makes the world better, as His grace pours out through them to bless the world. It is by standing firm in the faith and not denying their faith and their God that Christians can be Christ-like. It is by understanding and accepting that to live to God's way might at times call for sacrifice, suffering and persecution that each one can confront evil and overcome it.

Just as the brave and holy martyrs of the past stood firm in their faith and love of God regardless of the cost, let us stand firm. Just as the martyrs raised their eyes to heaven and cried 'Your will not mine', let us do the same. Just as the martyrs confronted in love the evil the world tried to force upon mankind. Let us do the same.

Now is the time for all Christians to stand up and be counted for Christ. Now is the time for all Christians to say 'Enough'. Now is the time for all Christians to support those leaders who are truly Christian, not those who claim to be Christian but show by their words and action they are anti-Christian.

Let your voices be heard. Let your God smile upon you as He sees how strong your love for Him is as you raise your voice in love of Him.

United Oct 11, 2012

WITH THE world in so much turmoil let all of us unite in prayer that the peace of Christ, Our Lord, will fill all hearts, lives and societies. It is only in His peace that humanity can reach it's full potential and truly find happy and complete lives. Today the world sinks into the confusion, turmoil and uncertainty that comes with the accepting so many wrongs of evil and ignoring or rejecting the truth of God. Today a blanket of darkness covers many and blinds many to the true way of life in Christ, Our Lord. Because of this so many suffer. Lives, families and civilizations are torn apart and the world seems not to be able to find the answer to solve all of this.

We as followers of Jesus are duty bound to make every effort to change the world and lives by letting the world see His love in our lives and experience His grace through our lives. This means we have to follow the way Our Lord, Jesus, lived. This means we should be the bringers of peace to all just as He is. We have to pray for all as He did. We have to try and lead all onto the right path that leads to heaven, the path of Jesus. The same path Jesus has led us onto. We have to be prepared to sacrifice for all just as Christ sacrificed for all. We should have shoulders prepared to carry the crosses of others with lives willingly given in suffering for others.

We have to be the ones who shine brightly in the gentle love of Christ so as to remove the hatred of evil from the world. We have to walk as Christ walked with hearts open to all. We have to proclaim the truth of God to all and never waiver from that divine truth. We have to show the world that the answer to its problems is found in Christ, Our Lord. This is what we are called to do. This is what our lives are meant to be. This is who we are created to be. Today Our Lord, Jesus, asks of each one of us who love Him, 'Can you drink from this cup?' I pray I can and I pray you can so that together in the chalice of divine love we truly can imitate Our Lord and Saviour, Jesus Christ, and in doing so bring the world to its senses.

I also pray this will be your prayer for yourself and for others. May God fill you with every grace and blessing.

The Holy Time of Easter

Apr 3, 2012

IT WAS at the Holy time of Easter that The Lord, Jesus, showed how merciful and tender was His love for mankind. Even though He suffered terribly all He asked of The Father was mercy for mankind. Even though The Lord, Jesus, had all the power of God, he did not use that power to destroy those who abused Him. Instead, The Lord looked with tender love through His pain and saw the weakness of mankind and reached out to help people overcome their failings. With His gentle and divine heart open to all, The Lord accepted the suffering put upon Him so as to carry mankind's suffering through sin into the tomb with Him and raise mankind up in His resurrection offering them the grace to overcome sin in His divine sacrifice.

The Lord, Jesus, revealed to mankind the true nature of God, that which is love and mercy, that which is tenderness and forgiveness.

Many are blind to this and see God as an authoritarian God who demands from mankind and punishes severely those who do not obey His divine will on earth. Some see God as distant and to be feared. Yet, Jesus, in His life and in His death, showed this is not how God is. He reminded mankind with His Sacrifice that God is love. That God loves mankind and is prepared to give His all to save mankind. That God is merciful and forgiving. That God does not want mankind to suffer but wants mankind to be free of pain in Him. The Lord as a prisoner on the cross, exposed to all the way to true freedom from sin and evil so that mankind could live in the light of His love and be happy in life.

God did this because He loves mankind and wants to lift mankind up in His divine glory. Not because it makes God any greater but because it makes mankind greater.

The message of the cross is there for all to see and if all ask the Holy Spirit to truly see it then all will come to know the truth of God's love. The message of forgiving love, merciful love, suffering love, tender love and love that says to all I am here for each one of you.

Christmas Message Dec 15, 2012

IN THIS blessed time of the year where many, even though they may not recognize it, are part of the celebration of the birth of Our Lord, Jesus. As every time people say, 'Merry Christmas', they are proclaiming the joy of the birth of The Lord. Let us, who know and love Christ, make the words 'Merry Christmas', a prayer for those we say them to. Let us in those words place the emphasis on Christ and let our internal prayer be that those who hear the word Christmas are touched by Christ's love through it.

Hoping that in doing so we may bring Christ into the life of the person so that they may be born anew in Him and His Holy Catholic Church. This is the greatest gift we can give and offer to others. This is the true spirit in which the words are meant to be spoken, The Holy Spirit, that brings merriment into the hearts of people as they are touched by the love of Our Lord and Saviour, Jesus Christ. As we look to the Infant Jesus, let us go to all in child like love bringing the Holy Child with us and through us into the lives of others

Whenever God Touches a Life Feb 4, 2013

WHENEVER GOD touches a life it always has been and always will be with and in love, for He is love. The life touched by His divine love is never the same again as the knowledge of God's love drives the person to be a better person. Even though some do not succeed as they are tempted away by evil, still inside their heart is that knowledge that God loves them and the hope is that in the future the strength of that divine love will overcome the weakness of the persons pride or fear.

It is when the people of the church see those who have been touched by God's love reach out and help the person to embrace and come to know God's love in the catholic faith and in the sacraments that it is less likely someone will fall away. God's love always needs to be nurtured and strengthened in life. This is something a person cannot do alone. Everyone needs the help of others to look for and find the grace that God offers in His catholic church and in the sacraments. It is therefore the duty of those within the church to look to always helping others especially those who have newly discovered God's love and been touched by His love.

It at times is so tempting to turn away and say let someone else do this. It is so easy to think only of your own faith growing and your own journey with God. However, unless we help others our faith will not grow and our journey will be more with self than with God.

The evil one works on peoples pride and self-centredness to draw them away from the life they truly should be living for God. A life of serving God and serving others. A life focused on God and bringing others to God. The Divine Spirit of Love is touching many hearts and souls in these times, just as He has always done. God hopes that those who know His love will know that it is they that are called to strengthen those who are newly experiencing His divine love. It is they who are called to fertilize the new of faith so that they can become a blazing fire of God's love and become the fire that set alight God's love in the lives of others that they know. The Lord is sowing the seed in many lives and he asks His followers to nurture the crop and harvest it in His love. Will we do as God calls us to do or will we turn away letting others do what we should?

I Am Love

Mar 28, 2013

THE LORD, Jesus, opened His heart in suffering love on the cross. He cried out in and through the pain His love for mankind. Imploring all to come to Him in love so as to receive His divine forgiveness. He called in tenderness, 'Come to Me', asking nothing in return except that mankind does its best to love Him.

The Lord's words echo throughout time reaching out to every heart and soul. His words filled with pain for the sins of mankind and filled with love for the forgiveness of mankind.

High upon the hill hanging on the cross God's only Son showed to mankind the depth and truth of God's love. As His flesh tore on the nails, as His body was racked with pain, as the thorns bit into His holy skin, as the pain of each breath filled Him still He looked upon mankind with love even though it was and is mankind who caused His suffering. He looked and cried tears of love for every soul that would be lost in the darkness as they refused His love and tears of joy for every soul saved by His sacrificial love as they embraced Him in love. On the cross Jesus showed to all those who would look with opened hearts I AM love and I AM here for you and because of you. Then when He was placed in the darkness of the tomb Jesus took all of our sins with Him so that we could in Him bury our sins and be brought into the light of His love as He rose from the dead. Death could not contain Him, Hell could not restrain Him or overcome Him. Instead He illuminated the dark, He defeated death, He broke the power of Hell and all evil. He said to mankind find victory in me, leave your sins in the darkness where they belong and let my resurrective light bring you to rise to a new life in Me.

This Easter let us rise in Christ, Our Lord, shining in His divine love. Giving thanks to God for the greatest love mankind ever has or ever will see in His Son, Jesus. Let us take to all Our Risen Lord, so that others may find His love through us and rise to eternal glory in His love.

Jesus showed us how to open our hearts in love let us not be afraid to do so. Let us show we truly embrace our suffering and risen Lord, Jesus, by the way we open our hearts in love to all regardless of what it may cause us to suffer.

He is with us Jun 8, 2013

EVEN THOUGH the church does and will face many trials and tribulations it will always remain as a bastion of God's love and will never be overcome by the world. The world may assail the church with all it has but the One Holy, Catholic and Apostolic Church will never be overcome. God resides within His church and all the power of the world does not and cannot compare to the power of God's love.

We as members of the church, as the new disciples of Christ and as the Apostles of His love must never doubt this and always stand firm in the face of any and all attacks upon the Body of Christ, which we are part of, The Catholic Church. We must stand as Christ, Our Lord, calls us to; firm in the truth, gentle in love and forgiving to all.

Even when it seems as if all are against us remember God is with us encouraging each one of us to truly be His followers. Also remember the world opposed Him, many rejected Him and many were and are against Him. The Lord, is with us in our struggles, He helps us carry our crosses and He give us the grace, the gifts and the strength we need to do as He asks of us.

Our Lord, Jesus, does not leave us alone, He is with us and He sends His Divine Spirit to bless us and fill us with the peace of heart and soul we need.

God is with us who can overcome us? God is in our hearts who can break them? God fills our spirits with His Spirit so who can defeat us?

The truth is clear and we should live to that truth that we are God's vessels of grace through whom He desires to show His love to the world and to whom He sends His Holy Spirit so that we can show His love to all.

Do not be bowed down by the world. Do not hide your faith. Do not deny your Lord.

Raise your heads high in love, open your hearts in love and let your spirits soar in God's love.

He is with us and we need to be with Him.

Books available from:

USA

Alan Ames Ministry
PO Box 1281
Madisonville, Louisiana 70447

Web: www.alanames.org
Facebook: Alan Ames International Ministry

Australia

Touch of Heaven
(Alan Ames Ministry)
PO Box 85
Wembley, 6014
West Australia

Phone: 61 89275 6608
Web: http://www.alanames.ws
Email: touchofheaven@iinet.net.au